HOUSING THE POOR IN THIRD WORLD CITIES

HOUSING THE POOR IN THIRD WORLD CITIES

(Choice Behaviour and Public Policy)

KAMLESH MISRA
Centre for Social and Urban Research University of Pitttsburgh
Pitttsburgh, USA

Foreword by
O.P. MATHUR
Director
National Institute of Urban Affairs, India

CONCEPT PUBLISHING COMPANY, NEW DELHI 110059

ISBN 81-7022-412-8

First Published 1992

Published and Printed by
Ashok Kumar Mittal
Concept Publishing Company
A/15-16, Commercial Block, Mohan Garden
NEW DELHI 110059 (India)

Lasertypeset by
Microtech Advance Printing Systems (Pvt.) Ltd.
H-13, Bali Nagar
NEW DELHI 110015

FOREWORD

Shelter is a basic human need. Every person tries to build a shelter, a roof over his head, to create a home, a permanent base where a greater part of his life is spent.

Shelter can be natural or man-made. It is a living space protected from the vagaries of nature, animals, and other humans. When man builds his shelter, he not only builds just a cell but also creates a structure in his own image -- in accordance with his needs, family size, economic capacity, social status, cultural values, and personality. He builds the structure in a specific environmental setting which conforms or nearly conforms to what he considers ideal in a given situation. The shelter so built, is otherwise called a house.

"For the individuals or the family, the house is both shelter and symbol, physical protection and physiological identity of economic value and a foundation for security and self-respect" (Aroni, p. 4). For the society it represents cultural development and perhaps one of the highest civilisational achievements. The architecture, the design, the size, the plan, the facilities inside, the environment outside, the services (water, sewerage, waste disposal, lighting, health, education, marketing etc.) in their totality represent the quality of housing which in turn reflect the quality of life of the people.

The form of houses and housing characteristics change with the change in taste, needs, technology, economy and physical environment in general. Technological changes in particular make a lot of difference. They influence population distribution, production processes, social organisation and the whole range of values and ethos.

The Industrial Revolution produced large concentration of population in cities. Pre-industrial rural homes were spacious with large open spaces for work. Houses were built through self help and with the cooperation of neighbours and housing design reflected local climate and heritage. The industrial revolution changed all this. Cities grew in size. Population became mobile and the space for building became scarce. House was no longer an inherited structure. It no longer had history behind. It no longer represented the unique tastes and values of a family. It got standardised. It started representing the tastes and values of an acquisitive and highly fragmented society. Housing became a property to be bought and sold. And therefore, also an industry for mass production.

So long as housing was the private affair of a sedentary family which had the necessary means to build its own shelter, there was no housing problem as such. With urban industrialisation people congregated in large cities, population grew further, land for building became scarce and costly, and the cost of construction increased beyond the capacity of the common man. A house could no more be built by individuals particularly the low paid workers who left their ancestral homes to work in factories, commercial establishments, and expanding informal activities. Housing became a problem.

The past century and early part of the twentieth century witnessed the worst in living condition in European and American cities. The post-World War II economic recovery and prosperity however made a great difference. Massive investments were made in urban infrastructure and public housing projects. The situation improved so that housing is no longer the prime issue in these countries. It is the environment particularly of the CBD, the city centre which dominates the urban problematique of the developed world.

What happened in the early part of this century in Europe, has now come to the Third World countries. There is massive influx of rural population to large cities because these cities alone have some industrial base to offer employment both formal or informal. Most of the people who migrate are poor. They go to the city to use its resources and consume its services. They are too poor to contribute any thing to city's infrastructure. These cities are thus overburdened with consumers of service. The available housing stock and the related services are practically choked. They are not only inadequate, they have also become non-functional.

It is estimated that by the turn of the century the urban population of developing countries will be tripled. More than 50 per cent of the people would live in urban areas. The urban infrastructure which could take care of 2 to 4 per cent additional demand in housing, is now called upon to meet 12 per cent increase. 8-10 additional units per 1000 population would have to be built to cope up with the situation. Only 2 to 4 units are being actually built.

This has led to a huge backlog of housing stock. And this backlog is growing at the rate of 4 to 5 million units each year. According to the UNCHS Report on Shelter and Urbanisation (1990) 100 million people world-wide are estimated to have no form of shelter at all. Such houseless people combined with those who live in shanty towns and slums now form majority in almost all the cities of the developing world. The UN report on the achievements of the International Drinking Water Supply and Sanitation Decade (1989-90) estimates that 18.3 per cent of the urban population of developing countries have no access to water supply, and another 28.3 per cent remain unserved by sanitation. In Asia and the Pacific Region, population unserved by water supply is 23 per cent of the total population residing in urban areas and this proportion is as high as 35 per cent in case of sanitation. The important point to note is that although the proportions of unserved population registered a decline during 1981-90, the absolute numbers increased from 212.70 million to 243.70 million in the case of water supply and 292.08 million to 377.0 million in the case of sanitation.

When we look at the megacities of the developing countries, the situation becomes more alarming. These cities present the worst forms of visible poverty for example, slums and squatter settlements and unsanitary living conditions and, not-so-visible poverty such as the high rates of infant mortality and high degree of drop-outs from the primary stages of schooling. According to the UNCHS Report on Shelter and Urbanisation, in Cairo "the tombs in the city cemeteries are houses to hundreds of thousands of people who have nowhere else to go apart from their city of dead," and in India, the same report cites that half a million people will be forced to sleep on the streets of Calcutta and further 10,000 men, women and children will spend the night on the pavements of Bombay. The UNCHS Global Report on Human Settlements (1986) has pointed out that in Mexico, 40 per cent of the total population live in what were called the informal settlements. In Sao Paulo, this proportion is 32, in Manila 37, and in Ankara 51.

If we update these figures, it may mean seven million persons living in some form of uncontrolled or unauthorised settlements in Mexico city, up to two million people living in very sub-standard accommodation is Sao Paulo, three million people living in *bustees* and refugee settlements in Calcutta and another 25 million people in similarly blighted and unserved areas, and some 3.5 million slum dwellers living on about 8000 acres of Bombay's land. In Cairo, more than one million people reside in the City of Dead with many more sleeping in mosques. Close to two million inhabitants squat on 415 sites dotted through out the Manila urban region. This number does not include families living in legal but otherwise sub-standard housing. Nearly 2.6 million persons or 40 per cent of Karachi's population live in squatter settlements or "*katchi abadis*". Approximately one-half of Lima city population lives in inner-city (tuqurious), and another 25 per cent in squatter settlements (Pueblo Javanese).

The situation with regard to water and sanitation is more appalling. In Mexico City tap water reaches only 50 per cent of squatter settlements. More than 75 per cent of Jakarta population have no direct connection to piped water supply system. Some ten per cent of them depend on water vendors paying five times that of the piped water. Thirty five per cent of the population of Metro Manila who live outside the water distribution system either purchase water from private vendors or are served by ground water. Lower income groups at times spend three times more per month on water from vendors but consume less than a sixth as those with running water. An estimated 100,000 persons in Bangkok obtain water directly from canals and waterways that are grossly polluted by human waste and industrial effluents.

Of the 13 million people in Sao Paulo, 8.5 million are not served by sewage system. Cairo has no publicly organised domestic solid disposal system. Septic tanks serve only 25 per cent of city's population. Only about 11 per cent of Metro Manila population is served by piped sewage. In Delhi 70 per cent of population does not have access to water borne sewage. The proportion is 100 per cent in unauthorised colonies. In Karachi only 20 per cent of houses are served by sewage system.

The above problems had their ramifications for urban housing policies. Several policies were inunciated to ease up housing shortage. The major emphasis, however, was placed on new construction by public authorities like housing boards, etc., and private investors. Efforts were also made to improve and expand municipal services like water supply, sewerage, waste disposal, lighting etc. The houses built under these programmes were not within the reach of the poor. Even those who could afford, could not get, as the supply was too short. As regards the municipal services, not much could be done. With increasing population, the old systems needed renovation. That could not be done because of prohibitive costs. And unless the old system was replaced, not much could be done in areas where it did not exist before. As such the progress was tardy and the situation worsened.

Since 1970s special attention came to be paid to the housing needs of the poor who lived in slums and shanty towns. At first, slum clearance projects were launched under which thousands of people were shifted to the peripheral areas. This could give a facelift to the city. The 'garbage' was removed and dumped away from sight. This did not succeed. New migrants came no sooner the old ones left. The slums increased in number. Today, at least half of the Third World's urban population lives in slums.

Site and service projects were the next in line. Under this scheme, land was prepared, sites were allotted and basic facilities provided. The allottees were to build their houses out of their own savings often incrementally. These schemes were launched in all the mega cities of the Third World in 1980s. Barring aside a few success stories, the programme did not achieve its objectives. The market forces were against the poor. As soon as the site was allotted and some structure came into being, it was sold out to better income groups. The original allottees continued to be homeless.

Then came the slum upgrading projects which sought to improve the environmental conditions (water supply, drainage, latrines, paths and lanes etc.) and to give the security of tenure. These programmes are still on but they have failed to make any major dent in the problem. As the old slums are upgraded newer ones with much greater squalor are born over night.

What can then be done to improve the housing conditions in Third World cities? The answer appears to lie in better housing policies than those adopted so far. But better housing policies can do precious little, if the urbanisation process continues to be what it is at present. If rural millions leaving their hearth and home seek housing in large cities, there is no hope of solving this problem in the near future. As such the Third World cities have to live with the current housing shortages and problems for years, may be decades to come. But even if the population of the Third World cities is stabilised at 1992 level, the problem of housing the poor is serious and calls for new policies and strategies to tackle and resolve it. Unfortunately, the efforts made so far have not only been not commensurate with the gravity of the problem, but also half-hearted in implementation.

Dr. Kamlesh Misra's book on *Housing the Poor in Third World Cities* is a good attempt at understanding the parameters for housing policies in the Third World cities like Rio de Janeiro. Eventhough the book covers only selected dimensions of public behaviour and housing policy, it does attempt to explain why housing policies have not so far benefited the poor. What the people need; what can they afford; how do they choose a house, etc. are issues that must form *inter alia* the bases for formulating housing policies.

Dr. Misra has used logistic model to an empirical situation in Rio, Brazil to prove that unless the choice behaviour of the people is taken into account, the effectiveness of housing policies will tend to be minimised. It is true that as income increases people need bigger and better accommodation. But what is better and bigger has a wide range and varies from culture to culture and group to group. For example, the low income households prefer small houses with space for future expansion to large apartment. The above is a significant conclusion and points to a policy which allocates plots without transfer rights and a built in provision for immediate occupation. This would be the cheapest means of drastically reducing, if not eliminating housing shortage in Third World cities. These sites could be provided in the urban fringe. The other conclusions of the study are also to be examined for their relevance in other cities of the world. Above all, the importance of the book lies in the need to conduct similar and perhaps more broadbased studies elsewhere so that a truly meaningful housing policy can be evolved.

Broadly speaking, the problems of housing the poor in Rio de Janeiro are not very different from those in other Third World cities. The difference lies in details. Dr. Misra's book ably covers, eventhough only partially, these broad perspectives and breaks new grounds in both problem and policy analyses. It is highly relevant to urban housing issues in Third World countries. The Chapter on India makes this book pertinent to South Asian and Southeast Asian countries too as they have similar urban development problems.

OM PRAKASH MATHUR
Director,
National Institute of Urban Affairs

New Delhi
1 January, 1992

PREFACE

In the past quarter of a century, several developing countries have experienced rapid economic growth. Nevertheless, approximately 800 million people are without adequate food, shelter, and health care (Chatterjee, 1981). The World Bank projects that by the year 2000, there will be about 400 million city dwellers in developing countries living below an absolute poverty threshold (World Bank, 1980).

With the growth of cities, demand for housing has greatly increased in most developing countries. Policies directed towards improving the housing situation have not made any major dent in the problem. It is estimated that at least half of the urban population of these countries does not have liveable shelter.

While it is true that rapid increase in urban population and lack of investment resources are the two major sources of this problem, faulty forecasts of housing demand by policy-makers is no less an important cause for the widening gap between housing demand and supply in third world cities. For an accurate forecast, policy-makers have to have information on how the people choose a dwelling to live in; i.e. what variables affect peoples housing choice decision, they would be able to make better housing policies. Otherwise the resources might go to the projects which do not meet the needs of the people.

This book examines how households, given a set of socio-economic characteristics and faced with different types of housing, choose a certain type of dwelling to live in. It tries to identify the factors that go into housing decision-making process; uses logit analysis to estimate housing choice probabilities by different sectors of the population of Rio de Janeiro municipality; and makes significant policy recommendations for the provision of housing in third world cities like Rio.

Many people have contributed to my intellectual development in general and to the development of this book in particular. I am particularly thankful to Professor Barbara M. Fraumeni of Northeastern University and Professor Lata Chatterjee of Boston

University, who besides creating an inspiring and challenging research environment, got me interested in the housing choice decisions of households in Third World cities with focus on Rio de Janeiro. Professor Kamran Dadkhah and Professor Fred Luk went through the book when it was presented as a doctoral dissertation at Northeastern University, Boston.

The following individuals also deserve mention: Professor T.R. Lakshmanan at Boston University, Professor Jerry Hausman of Massachusetts Institute of Technology and Professor Catherine Keil of Northeastern University. They have had an enormous influence on my intellectual development and continue to be great providers of inspiration.

Some times during the problematic and tedious work I was helped by many people. These include Professor William Greene of New York University, William Goedicke of Centre for Labor Market Studies and Gustavo Aristizabal of Northeastern University. They were always available for discussions.

I am indebted to Professor Morris A. Horowitz and in particular the Department of Economics at Northeastern University for providing me with financial support with which to complete this work and, to Miss Jennifer L. Dawson for typing the manuscript and making several revisions on them.

Although the purpose of this study is intellectual it cuts across many emotional and practical aspects of life. This is where constant encouragement and support are most valuable. I do not pretend to capture the wealth of support I have enjoyed, but I just want to mention the most important sources. My friends include: Dr. Gopalan Kutty, Ms. Dene Tin Tun, Jennifer Clifford and Ms. Neeta Fogg. All have provided enormous support during my work.

I am grateful to my parents for inspiration and to my wife, Sadhana for enduring my hiding away during evenings and weekends. It has been wonderful to share this stage of life with her.

Lastly, I am thankful to Sri Ashok Mittal, Concept Publishing Company for taking up the publication of this book.

January 1992 KAMLESH MISRA

CONTENTS

LIST OF FIGURES

LIST OF TABLES

1

INTRODUCTION

Urban explosion and its consequences for human welfare and development have now become major concerns of national governments and international organisations. The problem has acquired serious proportions in the developing countries where the rural millions who migrated to large cities in search of work have remained shelterless for decades. Slums and squatter settlements have become the hall marks of Third World cities. The squalor and filth of these settlements is the same in Calcutta, Bangkok, Rio de Janeiro, Lagos or Cairo. Only their names are different — *Jhopadpattis*, Campungs, slums and *falloless*.

The causes of acute shortage of housing in Third World cities are many. One can capsule them into a single cause i.e. an unprecedented urban population increase. The urban population of the world almost tripled to **1.99 billion** (1985) in the past 35 years. While it doubled in the industrialised countries from 450 to 840 million, it quadrupled in the Third World countries from 285 million to 1.15 billion. Within a span of just 60 years (1920-80), urban population of developing countries increased tenfold. The rural population, in the same period, just doubled.

Rapid increase in urban population in countries whose economies have yet to cross the take-off stage has placed serious strains on urban infrastructure and housing stock. Both of these were in poor conditions, apart from being acutely inadequate, to begin with. With the urban explosion, the situation has gone out of control and has practically become unmanageable. Most of these countries are highly indebted. They do not have the capacity to effect improvements which are commensurate with the seriousness of the problems.

In the absence of any meaningful rural development effort, the people living in villages and hamlets have moved to the towns. Thus, the poverty which once was concentrated in rural areas, has now become urbanised. It has also become visible because it is no longer dispersed.

While all the cities, big or small, of developing countries suffer from housing shortage, the larger ones suffer most because their population has increased faster. In 1940, 12.5 per cent of the population of Third World countries was urban, and only one per cent lived in million or more cities. In 1980, 32 per cent of the population was urban and 10 per cent lived in cities of a million or more population.

Recent UN projections show that the rural population of Third World countries might reach an upper limit by A.D. 2015. Beyond this point any population growth will be in urban areas only. And by that time 50 per cent of the population of these countries will be urban. The urban population of Africa will double between 1985 and A.D. 2000. Asia will experience the highest absolute growth adding 500 million inhabitants to its already over crowded cities. Fifty per cent of the growth will come from natural increase and the remaining 50 per cent from rural-urban migration, integration of villages into expanding municipal boundaries and the changes in definition of settlements from rural to urban.

The metropolitisation process in the Third World countries can be better gauged from the fact that just three of the world's ten largest cities had more than a million population in 1960. By A.D. 2000, eight of the ten largest cities of the world will be in the developing countries. In 1960 Shanghai was the only city with 10 million inhabitants. By A.D. 2000 there will be 18 cities with 10 million inhabitants. In 1960, the Third World has nine cities with 4 million population; in 1980 the number went up to 22. By A.D. 2000 there will be 50 such cities and by 2025, the number will go up to 114, as the total of such cities would reach 135 in the world as whole.

No matter what the economic and social systems the governments of the Third World pursue, urbanisation with increasing concentration of population in large cities will continue unabated at least for another quarter of a century. Any new international or national initiative to stabilise rural population will not bear fruits in the short-run. The repercussions of the past policies encouraging rural-urban migration will continue to be felt for decades to come.

Cities and Development

Cities now play a major role in economic development in the Third World countries. And the metropolitan cities have a pride of place in the new urban-industrial dispensation. Cities produce more than 60 per cent of G.D.P. Lima with 27 per cent of Peru's population accounted for 43 per cent of G.D.P. in 1981; Lagos had only 5 per cent of Nigeria's population but accounted for 57 per cent of the total value added in manufacturing in 1978; Greater Sao Paulo, has only 10 per cent of Brazil's population but contributed 40 per cent of the total value added in manufacturing in 1980. The story of the other metropolises of developing countries is more or less the same.

While it is true that rural development could have a sobering effect on urbanisation, and urban problems, the experience of the past few decades hints at a double edged policy of integrated rural-urban development making rural areas benefit from urbanisation and urban areas benefiting from rural development. Treating urban centres as sore points in the spatial economy has done emense harm to the process of economic progress in the Third World countries. Clearly, the economies of scale found in the large cities make it possible for them to produce far more than their share of population. They also facilitate production by providing effective marketing, financial, distributional, infrastructural and other services.

> "There has been and will continue to be a close relationship between the level of urbanisation and the level of economic development. In 1988, for example, only about 35 per cent of the population in the lowest income developing countries (with per capita income below $480) lived in urban areas. In middle-income developing countries (with per capita income of $ 1930), 58 per cent of the population was urban. Nearly 62 per cent of the population in upper middle-income countries (per capita income $ 3240) lived in urban places. In high income developed countries (average per capita income of $ 17080), 78 per cent of the population lived in urban areas.
>
> The relationship between economic development and urbanisation are complex and mutually reinforcing. Instead, productivity in agriculture frees labour that migrates to cities in search of employment and economic opportunities, creating large and diversified labour forces that allow manufacturing and service sectors to expand. This growth, in turn, attracts more migrants to cities allowing greater economies of scale and agglomeration."[1]

Notwithstanding the above potentials, the rapid pace of

urbanisation in the Third World countries has led to serious social and economic problems which need urgent attention. These are:

1. Increasing urban poverty;
2. Concentration of modern economic activities in large cities forcing the rural population to emigrate;
3. Increasing pressure on urban services and infrastructure; and
4. Environmental degradation.

Housing in Third World Cities

Shelter provision is a major component of the UN programme of urban development in Third World countries. In 1976, the UN Conference on Human Settlements (Halbitat) made a series of recommendations. One of the major recommendations was that "national housing policies must aim at providing adequate shelter and services to the lower income groups, distributing available resources on the basis of greatest need". The governments clearly recognised the urgency of meeting low cost shelter needs.

"From the 1950s, however, governments in developing countries struggled with problems of providing housing, utilities, infrastructure, and health and educational services to bourgeoning urban populations. Five stages in the evolution of public policies in developing countries dealing with slums and squatter settlements are discernible. Initially, many governments tried to solve the problems through slum clearance and forced migration. Squatters were evicted from the land they had occupied illegally. The assumption was that squatter settlements were not a solution to the shelter problem and that such eviction would discourage others from illegally occupying government or private land.

A second stage in the evolution of housing programmes was public housing. Slums were cleared and public low-income housing schemes were implemented to resettle those people who were dislocated. The failure of public housing programmes to provide adequate shelter for the poor, led to a third stage in the evolution of housing policy, the provision of minimum services for existing slums and squatter settlements. This stage reflected a significant shift in government policy. The difficulty of eliminating squatter settlements was recognised and at least minimum basic urban services were provided.

The U.S. Agency of International Development's (USAID) Housing Guarantee Programme was a major source for financing low cost shelter. In the 1970s, this programme emphasised providing infrastructure for the urban poor through, *inter alia*, sites and services, slum upgrading and core housing. The programme guaranteed United States private sector loans to developing countries to finance shelter and urban development programmes. The programme authorised more than $2 billion in loan guarantees in more than 50 developing countries since 1962.

In the early 1970s, the World Bank also began financing urban shelter, community services and urban transport projects in developing countries. The urban shelter and community services projects were targeted toward low-income households. They focused on increasing the replicability of projects by increasing cost recovery, identifying affordable standards, and reducing subsidies, thereby improving shelter incrementally.

UNICEF also adopted guidelines during the 1970s for providing services for children in urban slums and shanty towns. UNICEF emphasised the need to identify new approaches to providing urban services and to developing special urban projects that were to include urban services.

UNICEF followed four principles in its urban basic services approach: first, community groups and individuals had to be involved in planning and implementing projects; second, services provided at the community level had to be simple and low cost; third, community workers had to be selected by the community, have the support of the government personnel and be given simple training to undertake project activities; and, finally, planning and implementation of urban services had to reflect special features of both low-income urban communities and the urban environment.

During the 1980s, governments in most developing countries began to recognise the legitimate role of slums and squatter settlements in urban development. At this stage, the social and economic functions of squatter settlements were better known and upgrading was seen as a viable solution to urban service deficiencies. As a result, international support for shelter programmes significantly increased over the years. UNCHS executed many shelter projects. Four initiatives of the Commission on Human Settlements increased awareness concerning shelter and advocated strategies to respond effectively to settlement issues. These included the International Year of Shelter for the Homeless, the Global Report on Human Settlements, 1986, "A New Agenda for Human Settlements" and the Global Strategy for Shelter to the year 2000.

During the past three decades, developing countries have also formulated and implemented new policies and programmes to increase the access of the urban poor to shelter and services. In some countries, governments also enacted programmes to provide access to land for shelter, especially by granting security of land occupation to squatters and to increase the access of the urban poor to the financial institutions and encourage domestic savings for housing improvements. In other countries, policies and programmes were designed to elicit participation of poor households in planning, implementing and evaluating shelter projects. Public responses to the problems included programmes for improving cost recovery of government investments; for ensuring that government sponsored housing programmes were affordable; and for modifying building codes and standards, appropriate technologies, and building materials."[2]

Housing is thus one of the most serious problems of Third World cities. The poor who migrate to cities do not have the capacity to build or buy a house. They are used to live in traditional houses, huts, or even shacks in rural areas. Because of the wide open space, this does not create any major environmental problem. But when the same shacks are illegally built in cities, it leads to a variety of urban problems. The tragedy is that a great number of people have no access to even slums and squatter settlements. They spend their life on footpaths, in parks, in sewage pipes, and on sloppy and marshy lands.

The formal housing sector both private and public does not produce more than one-fifth of new housing stock in Third World cities. The remaining four-fifths is produced informally with various degrees of illegality, ranging from the unlawful occupation of land to the pervasive neglect of building codes, infrastructure standards, and zoning regulations for landuse and subdivision. During the early 1980s just one formal housing unit was added to the total urban housing stock of every nine new households in the low-income developing countries. The great bulk of the growing urban population is thus being housed in unauthorised informal settlements.

About 18 per cent of Bangkok population lives in informal settlements. The percentage for Abidjan is 20, for Karandi 35; for Bombay 38, for Mexico City 44; for Alexandria, 67 and for Dar es Salam 76 per cent. Over crowding is serious in inner city slums, where the supply of unauthorised housing has been severely curtailed and where rent control legislation discourages new rental units. In Kumagi, Ghana three out of every four households have only one room to live in. Half the population of Mexico City and most people in urban Africa live in such conditions.

Policy Alternatives

While the United Nations and other international agencies can help to improve the situation, the progress towards shelter for all will depend squarely on the national policies which directly and indirectly influence housing stock renewal and expansion. Experiences of the past five decades now make it abundantly clear that given the rapid increase in population, and the inability of the rural sector to provide income and job opportunities at a level the urban sector can, the current process of urbanisation cannot be halted in the short and medium run. Also given the economic crisis in which the governments of the Third World countries are today, the housing needs of the people without the participation of the beneficiaries on the one hand, and the private sector on the other cannot be met. Recent attempts in many developing countries to change the rent control laws and to encourage the private sector to invest in housing on a big scale is, therefore, a welcome step.

In order that the renewed efforts of governments and private sector in the developing countries make some headway, it is important to know the nature of the housing stock that people need. People consist of several segments and each one needs and demands a particular type of house. The institutional housing created in Third World cities caters to needs of the upper middle segment of the society. It has very little, if at all, to offer to the poor. Even if the private sector is brought into the picture, some of the questions remain unresolved. One of them is the implication of the choice behaviour of the people for housing policy.

Unless some reliable data are available on the choice behaviour, the housing policies may produce stock which might not be opted by the people. There are other research issues too which need attention. This book centres on the choice behaviour and its implications for urban housing policies.

Objectives of the Study

This study seeks to explain how households, given a set of socio-economic characteristics faced with different types of housing will choose a certain type of dwelling to live in. It tries to identify those factors that go into this decision making process. The study assumes that households derive utility from the characteristics of the house, and different households place different valuation to these attributes, depending on the characteristics of the decision-maker. In a sense, the socio-economic variables in the model are expected to capture the taste variation among the households.

The main objectives of this study can be put into four major groups:

1. To identify in a detailed manner the relative importance of the determinants of housing choice decisions in a developing country;
2. To identify variation in housing choice by different household classes;
3. To identify the differences in the importance of the determinants of housing choice between developed and developing countries, through comparison of existing research;
4. To suggest policies for improving the housing conditions in Rio; and
5. To indicate the relevance of the study to other developing countries like India.

This study identifies the role of different socio-economic variables like income, age, race, education, and occupation in the decision-making process, These variables are important in any housing choice study because they capture the taste variations for housing among different household classes. It also identifies and investigates why different households choose different housing and what role is played by socio-economic variables in the decision-making process. These two above-mentioned outcomes will be helpful in indicating future developments in housing demand by housing type in the Third World cities like Rio de Janeiro.

NOTES

1. UNDP, *The Challenge of Urbanisation: UNDP Urban Development Assistance Strategy for the 1990's*, Mimeographed, p. 5.
2. *Ibid.*, pp. 14-15

2

GENERAL THEORETICAL CONSIDERATIONS

Introduction

The major problem faced by an analyst in choice analysis is the modelling of choice from a set of mutually exclusive and collectively exhaustive alternatives. This study of housing choice analysis uses the Principle of Utility Maximisation. A decision-maker is thought of as selecting the alternative with the higher utility among those available at the time the choice is made. In order to make the choice model operational, the utility function must have as arguments, observable independent variables whose associated parameters can be estimated from a sample of observed choices made by the decision-makers.

In practice, it may be impossible to specify and estimate a choice model that will always be correct in predicting the chosen alternative by all individuals. In order to overcome this problem we resort to the concept of random utility. In a random utility model the true utilities of any alternative are considered as random variables. Thus, the probability that an alternative will be chosen is defined by the probability that it has the highest utility amongst the available alternatives.

In order to understand any theory of choice four major elements need to be defined they are:

The Decision-Maker

A unit of decision-making can be an individual or a household. Individuals face different choice situations and have widely different tastes, thus, any study must explicitly treat the differences in decision making processes among individuals. The model to be used should be able to capture major taste variations among households.

Alternatives

A choice is, by definition, made from a set of available alternatives at the time of decision-making. The constraints and the environment of the decision-maker determines the set of available alternatives or the choice set. The choice set must consist of alternatives that are feasible and available to the decision-maker during the decision process.

Attributes of the Alternatives

The attractiveness or unattractiveness of an alternative is evaluated in terms of a vector of attribute values. Since we assume that alternatives are heterogeneous, the decision-maker can evaluate different attributes and different decision-makers can assign different values to the same attribute of the same alternative.

Decision Rule

In a situation of choice, a decision rule describes the internal mechanism used by the decision-maker to process the information available and arrive at a unique choice (Ben-Akina and Lerman, 1987). The decision rule used in this study is based on the concept of utility. Here the attractiveness of an alternative is expressed by a vector of attribute values. There exists an objective function expressing the attractiveness of an alternative in terms of its attributes. This index of attractiveness is what we refer to as utility. The index is based on the notion of compensating offsets. For a household faced with four choices and their respective utilities being U_1, U_2, U_3 and U_4. The decision-maker will choose the alternative with the highest utility.

Much has been written and debated over in the literature as to the appropriateness of different models of housing choice studies. However, all models of housing choice are based on two strands of theory which I am using as a theoretical basis for the model that I plan to estimate in the latter stage of the study. We use two strands of theory namely some extension of the developments in consumer theory and the developments in discrete choice theory. The relevant extensions of traditional consumer theory include the emphasis on micro data. Also consumer demand models have been enriched with exogenous socioeconomic variables which have been found to improve explanation.

The developments in consumer theory that we look into are the household production approach and discrete choice theory. The household production approach defines utility in terms of characteristics of goods, which is very appealing, when the characteristic in question is only indirectly demanded as in the case of housing.

Extensions of Traditional Consumer Theory

Consumer theory is formulated for individual households. Thus, there are no obvious grounds why the theory should be directly applicable when data for aggregates of households is used. Recently, however, microdata sets have been made available in many developing countries, which makes it possible to apply microeconomic theory without aggregation bias.

It has also been found that socio-economic variables need to be included if traditional consumer theory is to explain variations in demand. More recently, ways of incorporating socio-economic variables into demand models have been developed. Awon, Odling-Smee and Whitehead (1982) developed a model to test the hypothesis that household characteristics such as size, occupation, and education affect housing demand. The household characteristics are supposed to affect the utility associated with particular dwelling attributes.

Household Production Theory

Traditional consumer theory maximises utility, a function of goods, subject to budget constraint. When the system is solved for quantities of goods demanded, demand is a function of price of goods and the income of the consumer. The household production approach analyzes the role of goods more carefully. One line of household production theory was presented by Becker (1965). Consumer combine market goods and time into commodities from which utility is derived.

Another line in which we are more interested here was introduced by Lancaster (1966a) and Muth (1966). The basic idea is the same in both contributions. According to this approach, utility is derived from the services that a household produces using the goods that are purchased or in other words, from the characteristics of the goods. Consumption is an activity in which goods are inputs and in which the output is a collection of characteristics. Utility or preference orderings are assumed to rank collections of characteristics and only to rank collections of goods indirectly through the characteristics that they possess. Intuitively appealing as the approach is, it is not without its problems. For one, it assumes linearity and divisibility. For durable, expensive goods divisibility is not a realistic assumption. Rosen (1974) assumes indivisibility and states the model directly in terms of prices and quantities of characteristics.

Probabilistic Choice Theory

The development of choice theories arose from the need to explain experimental observations of inconsistent and non-transitive preferences. Probabilistic choice mechanisms were introduced to explain the behavioural inconsistencies. The inconsistencies can arise when we observe the choice made by a sample of individuals in which two or more individuals with identical choice sets, attributes, and socio-economic characteristics select different alternatives. Here we make use of Random Utility Theory to explain choices.

Random Utility

The random utility approach introduced by Manski (1977) has been more in line with consumer theory. The observed inconsistencies in choice behaviour are assumed to be a result of observational deficiencies on the part of the analyst. The individual is always assumed to select the alternatives with the highest utility. However, the utilities are not known to the analyst with certainty and are therefore treated by the analyst as random variables. From this point of view the choice probability of alternative *i* is equal to the probability that the utility of alternative *i*, U_{in}, is greater than or equal to the utilities of all the other alternatives in the choice set. That is:

$$P_{in} = (U_{in} \geq U_{jn})$$

In this approach choice probabilities are derived by assuming a joint probability distribution for the set of random utilities. The underlying idea of this distribution assumption is based on the underlying sources of the randomness of the utilities. There are four distinct sources of randomness as captured by the model.

Unobserved Attributes: The vector of attributes affecting the decision is incomplete therefore, the utility function,

$$U_{in} = U(Z_{in} + \varepsilon_{in}, S_n)$$

Includes Z^{U}_{in}, which is observationally a random variable consequently the utility is itself random.

Unobserved Taste Variations: The utility function $U_{in} = U(Z_{in}, S_n, S_n^{U})$ may have an unobserved component, S_n^{U} which varies among individuals. Since S_n^{U} is unknown the utility is U_{in} a random variable.

Measurement Error: It is possible that the utility function is:

$$U_{in} = U(Z_{in}, S_n)$$

and the attributes of Z_{in} are not observable, we observe Z_{in} which is an imperfect measure of Z_{in}. That is,

$$Z_{in} = Z_{in} + \varepsilon_{in}$$

Where ε_{in} is unknown measurement error. Thus, our utility function now becomes:

$$U_{in} = U(Z_{in} + \varepsilon_{in}, S_n)$$

In general, we can express the random utility function of an alternative as a sum of observable and unobservable components as:

$$U_{in} = V(Z_{in}, S_n) + \left(S^{U_{in}}, S^{U_n}\right) = V_{in} + \varepsilon_{in}$$

or,

$$P_{in} = Pr(V_{in} + \varepsilon_{in} \geq V_{jn} + \varepsilon_{jn})$$

The model which emerges from the above discussion is based only on the assumption we make about the joint probability distribution of the full set of disturbances. This will be discussed in detail in the modelling chapter.

—

3

SURVEY OF LITERATURE

Introduction

In the past a wide variety of housing market models have been developed and applied. The diversity of these models reflects the heterogeneity of the housing market itself. Consequently, a clear overview of the main research developments can hardly be given without ambiguity. Though many possibilities exist to classify these developments, however, we will restrict the survey to an overview of the research on residential choice, i.e., basically demand-oriented approaches in which elements like supply, price, etc. usually play a definite role, but are not starting points for analysis.

There are many different ways of looking at the housing market. Consequently, when the term housing market is used it is meant as a conceptual framework, within which a variety of processes can be identified. "It is a complex phenomenon of a whole variety of interrelated and mutually influencing sub-markets."[1]

The multidimensional nature of the housing market explains the diversity of development patterns with changes in settlement systems all over the world. This reflects changes in economic conditions, technological developments, demographic changes, social developments, the impact of public policy, etc. (Goldberg and Chinloy, 1984).

The stream of research on housing choice arose out of a broad base of research in housing economics that applied household production theory. Especially important in this respect are the theories of consumer behavior (Lancaster, 1966)[2] and hedonic analysis to evaluate the way in which attributes of housing influence demand.

A brief review of literature on housing choice indicates that models can be based on several theoretical frameworks. Knowledge of the most important theories can provide valuable information for any choice process, since most theories are strongly related to specific sets of models. Based on the literature review we can identify four different theoretical approaches under which models have been constructed for various choice situations. Namely: Behavioural Approaches, Economic Equilibrium Approaches, Heuristic Approaches, and Statistical Approaches.

Behavioural Approaches

The Behavioural Approaches are based on the motives and attitudes of decision-makers. Behavioural Approaches can be classified into three main classes: the Traditional Approach, the Revealed Preference Approach, and the Stated Preference Approach.

The Traditional Approach aims at explaining choice behaviour on the basis of the classical assumption of rational behaviour and perfect information. Usually the choice criteria in micro-economic decision-making underlying a traditional approach are assumed to be the same for all individuals, although the shape of the individual utility functions are not necessarily the same. Consequently, the same set of attributes of a choice alternative or the same set of commodities will not normally lead to the same utility for all individuals. The drawback of this approach is that consumer interactions are normally neglected, rational decision-making with perfect information is usually impossible, interpersonal utility comparisons are not possible and often no insight is given into the distribution of alternative choices over the population. Consequently, the result of this approach tends to have an aggregate (macro) character, despite the micro economic basis. Linear programming models (Alonso, 1984) have been used to implement the Traditional Approach.

The Revealed Preference approach aims at analyzing realized, single, and complex choices by means of disaggregate information on past behaviour. This information is usually derived from interviews [see, Pirie (1976) and Rushton (1969, 1971)]. The basic assumption of this approach is that human preferences can be inferred *a Posteriore* from the results of actual decisions. This approach also has several limitations: the mental process of consumers is neglected, uncertainties, habits, expectations, and constraints in choices are generally left aside. Models generally used under this approach are:

Conventional Random Utility and Discrete Choice Models

This is mainly based on a logit formulation. It uses data from pre-defined questionnaires (see, Ben-Akiva, 1973; Domencich and McFadden, 1975; McFadden, 1978; Amemiya, 1978; and Pitfield, 1984).

Adaptive Random Utility Models

The characteristics of the Adaptive Random Utility Model is like the family of general extreme value models (McFadden, 1978) and multinomial probit models (Daganzo, 1979). These models aim to especially include more choice options and more qualitative aspects of individual choice behaviour than the conventional random utility models. Among other things, they allow a more flexible specification. These models have become more important tools in the Behavioural Approach to modelling choice decisions.

The Stated Preference Approach

This approach analyzes choices and choice process *ex-ante* by means of information on *ex-post* expected utilities, i.e., information on the preferences of the choice makers and on their perceptions of the various alternatives. Owing to its ability to treat individual preferences and perception data, this stated approach is usually a disaggregate approach. It has the potential to deal with preferences for future choices, not yet in existence, and to take into account the mental images and processes of the decision-maker. This Approach, although intuitively appealing, is not yet entirely perfect.

Economic Equilibrium Approach

These approaches are rooted in the macro-economic theory of markets and can be considered macro adaptations of the traditional micro behavioural approach. In a given spatial system, they aim at finding partial equilibrium solutions for various types of separate special interactions. These partial equilibrium models have yielded the most robust conclusions. Examples of work in this area are Mills (1972) the general urban economic equilibrium formulation of Takayama and Judge (1972).

Given the focus of the study, we approach the survey by concentrating on models that have generally adopted the behavioural approach. This should provide a better understanding of the model to be used in the empirical part of this research.

An important development in modelling individual behaviour during the past fifteen years is the focus on models, which are basically explanatory, follow the behavioural approach and can process qualitative and quantitative data. This has led to the development of what are called Discrete Choice Models. In the next few sections a review of various disaggregate model is presented and their developments are discussed.[3] Disaggregate Models can be classified into (1) Deterministic Models and (2) Probabilistic Models. Deterministic Models are models in which the utility functions are supposed to give an exact description of the alternatives. Formally the derivation of the preferred alternatives is essentially a mathematical logical conclusion, from which uncertainties inherent in any choice situation are eliminated. Aggregation to class or population total presupposes that all individuals are faced with the same identical utility functions.

In Probabilistic Choice Theory the choice process of individuals can be described by a straight-forward mathematical programming procedure, which defines the probability of a specific choice. The Theory (for which the Post-1973 work of McFadden is extremely important) is related to the hedonic price problem in econometrics. The probability that certain decisions will be made partly depend on the observable attributes. In some models elements which are not directly observable also play a role. In others, however, the choice probabilities may even be influenced by the mutual relationships between alternatives. In other words, this approach does not imply that similar attributes lead to identical choices. From this group of models, random utility models will be discussed in greater detail due to their relevance to the current research. The description of the models presented is not entirely exhaustive, but the most recent important developments are reviewed, with the main emphasis on the underlying assumptions and model specification.

Deterministic Models

Logit Models

If it is assumed that the relevant utility functions are all exhaustive, we find among the group of deterministic disaggregated models the well known logit model; we define in this case the choice-ratio of any individual n for any alternative i compared to all other alternatives as:

$$P_{in} = \frac{U_{in}}{\sum_{i'=1}^{I} e^{u_{i'n}}}; i, i' = 1, \cdots I; i\, i'; n = 1 \cdot\cdot, N$$

with

P_{in} being the choice ratio of individual n for alternative i compared to all other alternatives

U_{in} being the utility of alternative i for individual n. U_{in} is based on $U(X_{in})$, a utility function of a vector X_{in} of explanatory, non-stochastic variables X_{jin} $(j=1 \; .. J)$. J is the number of variables j that definite alternative i for individual n. In the deterministic model two special assumptions are made concerning $U(X_{in})$

(1) The set of choices $i=1, \ldots I$ is exhaustive;
(2) Usually $U(X_{in})$ is defined by the following straight forward linear form

$$U(X_{in}) = \sum_{j=1}^{J} X_{jin}$$

Further the following condition should hold:

$$\sum_{i=1}^{I} P_{in} = 1$$

An important hypothesis, which makes the deterministic logit model possible is the Independence from Irrelevant Alternatives (IIA) Property. This Property states that the relative ratio of choices among two particular alternatives is not influenced by introducing other choice options. "The advantage of Independence from Irrelevant Alternatives is that the model is easy to handle in terms of estimating and forecasting" (Wal Van Lierop 1985, pp. 66). A disadvantage of this Property is that if a third alternative very similar to one of the already existing alternatives is taken into consideration, it is very difficult to make good sense of the various choice ratios. Consider for example the classic red-bus blue-bus problem. Suppose there is a traveller who has a choice of going by auto or taking a blue-bus and that both alternatives have the sample representative utility, since the representative utilities are equal, the choice probabilities are equal ($P_a = 1/2 = P_{bb}$) and the ratio of probabilities is one ($P_a / P_{bb} = 1$).

Now suppose that a red-bus were introduced and that the traveller considered the red-bus to be exactly like the blue-bus. Thus the ratio of probabilities of taking the two different coloured buses is one ($P_{bb} / P_{rb} = 1$). However, since in the logit model the ratio P_a / P_{bb} is the same, independent of the existence of the other alternatives, this ratio remains constant at one. The only probabilities for which $P_a / P_{bb} = 1$ and $P_{bb} / P_{bb} = 1$ are $P_a = P_{bb} = P_{rb} = 1/3$, which are the probabilities that the logit model predicts. In real life, we would expect the probability of taking an auto to remain the same when a new bus is introduced that is the same as the old bus. We would also expect the original probability of taking a bus to be split after a new bus is introduced, between the two buses, i.e., we would expect $P_a = 1/2$ and $P_{bb} = P_{rb} = 1/4$.

It should be mentioned here that it is very difficult if not impossible to solve completely the problem discussed above within the framework of the logit model — because the axiom of IIA is one of the main assumptions of the logit model.

Gravity and Entropy Models

Utility-based gravity and entropy models[4] have sometimes been regarded as deterministic models of choice (see Wilson, 1977 and Nijkamp, 1979). This type of a model has been justified where there exists a direct relationship between the entropy concept from information theory and the logit models (Van Lierop and Nijkamp, 1979). The basic feature of these models is the assumption that any spatial interaction is the result of three forces:

(1) Attraction at a point of origin;
(2) Attraction at a point of destination; and
(3) Distance friction

On the basis of information about these three forces, the spatial flow pattern at the macro level can be assumed in a deterministic way. During the past fifteen years, these models have gained much popularity in urban and regional science due to their relatively simple framework, but they are based on physical concepts and do not really explain spatial choice behavior. These models do have relation to the disaggregated models but cannot be fully representative of the class.

Probabilistic Models

The literature on Probabilistic Models follows a different direction of theoretical research. Probabilistic models include as subtopics:

(1) The Constant Utility Model; and
(2) The Random Utility Model

These approaches take the form of a variation on the basic logit concept. The derivation of the logit model in the Constant Utility Method is different from the more general Random Utility Method, thus, the discussion on these two approaches has to be independent.

Constant Utility Model

The basic assumption of this model is the choice axiom or IIA property as defined by Luce (1959).

Based on the fundamental assumption Luce (1959) proved that it is possible to define,

$$P_{in} = \frac{M_{in}}{\sum_{i'=1}^{I} M_{i'n}}; i, i' = 1 \ldots I; i \neq i'; n = 1 \ldots N$$

where

P_{in} = The choice probability that individual n will choose alternative i from a set of I available alternatives. In the Constant Utility Model the choice probability equals the proportion of the population whose choice for alternative i is determined by the same vector of explanatory attributes which is relevant to n.

M_{in} = A cardinal utility figure measured on a scale defined by all available alternatives I, and based on:

(1) The function of the vector of the relevant and perfectly described explanatory variables and

(2) The analytical way in which the Utility, resulting from the explanatory variables, is linked to the choice-probability by the internal probability 0 – 1.

The utility related to Point (1) under M_{in} is denoted by U_{in} is more or less the same as the deterministic logit model. In the deterministic logit model the related utility function, $U(X_{in})$, is assumed to be exhaustive. In the Constant Utility Model a less rigid, linear form is usually assumed for $U(X_{in})$.

$$U(X_{in}) = \sum_{j=1}^{J} \alpha_j X_{jin}$$

with α_j = a coefficient

The relationship between the model which describes the stochastic process by defining P_{in} and the deterministic utility U_{in} is made by an expression based on Point (2) under M_{in} for example

$$M_{in} = e^{U_{in}}$$

which after substitution gives us:

$$P_{in} = \frac{e^{U_{in}}}{\sum_{i'=1}^{I} e^{U_{i'n}}}; I \neq i'$$

This description shows that in the constant utility model only the process of choosing alternative i is stochastic, while the utility, U_{in}, itself is fixed and exactly defined.

To illustrate the connection with the deterministic logit model in a better way consider the following. Assume that the probability P_{in} is proportional to an arbitrary function G of the vector of explanatory variables: i.e.,

$$P_{in} = \beta_n G(X_{in})$$

where:

β_n = is a coefficient of proportionality

With this proportionality assumption the utility function does not depend on the actual choice model, as utility itself is constant..

Random Utility Approach

The Random Utility Approach is the most widely used approach in modelling individual choice process. This approach is based on two special features:

(1) It takes into account the fact that some of the characteristics of the alternatives and/or socio-economic attributes are often missing are unobservable to the researcher.
(2) It assumes that the individual decision-maker chooses an alternative under the condition of bounded rationality. Bounded rationally means that each individual maximizes utility rationally within the framework of personal criteria and a well defined structure of preferences which is reflected in personal utility functions. Some attributes, which are theoretically assumed to be very important, may not be included in the personal utility functions. Consequently, these elements of individual choice which are not included can lead to an unexplained part in the observed behavior.

The above two points indicate that different choices may be made by people who have exactly the same set of alternatives, described by exactly the same set of attributes, and that the choice has to be considered partly a *random decision*. Theoretically, these problems have been tackled by assuming that individual utility, on which the choice of specific alternative *i* is based, are random variables, based on a set of arguments of a *fixed* vector of explanatory variables, denoted by U_{in}. The connected utility function $U(X_{in})$, is a random function of these explanatory, alternative related, and/or socio-economic attributes. Thus,

$$U(X_{in}) = V(X'_{in}\beta) + \eta(X'_{in}) + \xi_{in}$$

where

β and γ are vectors of coefficients

$V(X'_{in}\,\beta)$ = is a deterministic function of the J' elements of the attribute Vector X_{in};

$\eta\,(X'_{in}\,\gamma)$ = a function of the following unexplained elements:

(a) individual taste variations with respect to the observed attributes;
(b) individual measurement error;
(c) possible inconsistencies in the individual's choice behavior; and
(d) the influences of the restrictive assumption of linearity of the strict utility function

ξ_{in} = a function of the influence on $U(X_{in})$ of omitted or purposely unobserved attributes.

In most empirical research it is impossible to separate the last two factors, thus they are always taken together as one disturbance term, ε_{in}, now we may write:

$$U(X_{in}) = V(X'_{in}\beta) + \varepsilon_{in};\ i=1;\ldots I;\ n=1\ldots N$$

In the random utility approach the maximizing process can be described as the evaluation process of individual *n* of the utility of all of the available alternatives, *i*, U_{in}. Thus, the probability that a random alternative *i* will be chosen by individual *n* is equal to the probability that the utility of *i* exceeds or equals the utility of any other alternative *i'* for *n*. For example, based on the work of McFadden (see McFadden, 1973), the fundamental equation of the random utility approach becomes,

$$P_{in} = Pr[U_{in} = Max(U_{i'n})] = Pr(U_{in} \geq U_{i'n'} \forall i')$$

$$P_{in} = Pr[V(x'_{in}\,\beta) + \varepsilon_{LV} \geq U(X'_{i'n}\,\beta) + 206_{i'n}]$$

$$Pr = [\varepsilon_{i'n} \leq V(X'_{in}\,\beta) + \varepsilon_{in} - V(X'_{i'n}\,\beta)]$$

In this type of an approach the calculation of choice probabilities depends on the form that is chosen for the above equations and, in the respect the distribution of the error terms ε_{in} plays a crucial role. The literature review indicates that several models can emerge from the

Random Utility Approach, each depending on the assumption one is willing to make on the distribution of the error terms. The models that will be discussed her follow the classification of Daganzo (see Daganzo, 1979).

Multinomial Logit Model

If we assume that the error terms are modelled by a set of variables which are mutually independent, identically extreme-value distributed,[5] and have zero mean, then they are uncorrelated with the directly measured attribute-values and the related parameters of the alternatives.

These requirements are met by a Weibull Distribution, which is a skewed distribution that can be almost normalized by using logarithms. In such a situation, Equation (1) reduces to the multinomial logit formula:[6]

$$P_{in} = \frac{e^{V(X'_{in}\beta)}}{\sum_{i=1}^{I} e^{V(X'_{i'n}\beta)}}$$

The above formula is to date the most widely used disaggregate demand model.[7] The reason for this seems to be that the model is relatively easy to interpret and its properties are generally well understood.

One of the most important properties of the MNL model is that the assumption concerning the probability distribution of the error terms introduces the same element again into the model, the IIA Property as has been discussed earlier. As Holman and Marley proved,[8] the choice axiom is theoretically equivalent to the assumptions about the distribution of the error terms in the fundamental equation of the random utility approach. What this means is that in the multinomial logit model, the relative probability of choice of two alternatives depends only on their measured attractiveness.[9] In cases where the unobserved components of alternatives (the errors) are correlated, the introduction of a new alternative which is highly correlated with another but which is only marginally inferior to it, will not affect the choice probabilities of all other available alternatives. It is thus highly unlikely that the new alternative will be chosen. When such relationships exist, the error terms assumptions of the MNL model may cause problems.

As has been pointed out by McFadden (1973), under such circumstances a solution may be try to capture the interdependencies between alternatives by defining adjusted specifications for the function $V(X'_{in}\ \beta)$. He, however, points out that this may be very difficult as it may require the introduction of a non-linear function. Some authors have tried to solve this problem by developing *ad hoc* corrections for the logit model.[10] We will discuss these models in the following pages.

Elimination by Aspects Method

Tversky (1972a, 1972b) developed a disaggregate choice method which makes use of the random utility concept, but is completely different from the methods described so far. The application of his model has mainly been in psychology. It does not concern itself about error terms or even assumptions about possible error terms.

The general assumption of the elimination by aspects (EBA) method is that the chooser selects an alternative in a sequential process based only on the known, identified, explanatory attributes or aspects. These aspects are scaled in order of importance and are to be interpreted as desirable features. The selection of a particular aspect leads to the elimination of all alternatives which do not contain this desired aspect.[11] The process terminates with the decision based on the last relevant aspect. With the decision the final choice is made.

Sequential or Multi-Level Logit Model

A practical way of dealing with the choice axiom, inherent in the use of MNL model, is the introduction of Multilevel Logit Models.[12] This approach is in line with the hierarchical elimination method.[13] By splitting the choice problem into several process stages, conditional choice probabilities are created. Part of the difficulty caused by the choice axiom can be solved by the systematics introduced into the model in this way. This is because, by using a sequential approach, the number of choice situations, available alternatives and parameters in each successive stage, decline rapidly. Another advantage of this method is that the estimation results are hardly affected compared to the direct estimation of the model.

A good illustration of the sequential logit model can be given by a spatial distribution problem in which a combined choice has to be made for Location Y and housing type Z. Assume P_Y/Z_n is the probability that a certain location will be chosen by an individual n when the housing type is already given, as well as the marginal probability P_{zn} for that housing type.

It is supposed that at first Z is chosen and only then Y. Furthermore, the assumption must be made that:

$$U(X_{zyn}) = A(X_{zyn}) + B(Z_{zn})$$

defines the total utility of the sequential approach choice problem. Where:

$A(X_{zyn})$ is a random utility subfunction based on a vector of directly observable variables, which vary in regard to both location choice Y and housing type, Z.

$B(X_{zn})$ is a random utility subfunction based on a vector of exploratory variables important to person n which vary only in regard to housing type Z. Thus, within the framework of the MNL Model the result is that only variables important to person n which vary only in regard to housing type Z are included. Thus within the framework of the MNL model the result is:

$$P_Y/zn = e^{A(X_{zyn})} / e^{W_{zn}}$$

$$P_{zn} = e^{B(X_{zn}) + W_{zn}} / \sum_{z'=1}^{z} e^{B(X_{z'n}) + W_{z'n}}$$

where: W_{zn} = Inclusive values defined as:

$$W_{in} = \ln\left[\sum_{y=1}^{Y_z} e^{A(X_{zyn})}\right]$$

A complete derivation of this model is provided in McFadden, (1978).

Although the above model has a good record of explaining actual choice behaviour, a problem with this multi-level logit model is that it may be inconsistent with utility maximization.

An empirical generalization of the sequential or multi-level logit model is the so-called nested logit model. Due to its relevance in our current research, this model will be discussed in some detail. Much of the review of this model will follow the outline presented by Axel Borsch-Supan.[14]

Nested Logit Model

An important and intuitive generalization of the MNL specification is the nested multinomial logit (NMNL) model (McFadden, 1978). One of the special features of this model is that it allows for substantial deviations from the "Independence of Irrelevant Alternatives" Assumption while retaining most of the computational advantages of the MNL Model. Presently the NMNL model is the most favourable compromise between the ideals of functional flexibility and computational ease. Applications of the NMNL model have been in transportation economics (the very first application seems to be Domencich and McFadden, 1975; Ben-Akiva and Lerman, 1985; and Train, 1986). Application to housing related problems are discussed in the works of Anas (1987), Cameron (1984), Borsch-Supan (1985, 1986, and 1987), and Fischer and Aufhauser (1986). The discussion that follows is a general discussion of the model which has been applied to housing and transportation economics.

Hierarchical Choice

The model is based on a multi-level hierarchy of groups of alternatives into subset of choices that are more alike to each other than relative to any other alternative.

In a two-level nested multinomial logit model, the I alternatives are grouped in K subsets, each consisting of I_k alternatives. The choice can be visualized as first among the K subsets, and then among the I_k alternatives in the chosen subset K. Thus, we may be able to decompose the choice probabilities as:

$$P_i (V) = Q_k (V) . P_{i/k} (V) \tag{1}$$

Where Q_k denotes the marginal choice probability of subset K and $P_{i/k}$ the conditional probability of choosing alternative i among the I_k alternatives in subset K. Q_k and $P_{i/k}$ have the functional form of simple multinomial logit choice probabilities.

$$P_i(V) = \frac{\exp(V_i/\theta_k)}{\exp(INC_k)} \cdot \frac{\exp(\theta_k INC_k)}{\sum_{j=1\ldots k} \exp(\theta_j INC_j)} \tag{2}$$

where:

$$INC_k = \log \sum_{i=J_k}^{JK+I_k-1} \exp(-V_i/\theta_k) \tag{3}$$

INC_k are called "inclusive value" of subset K. The summation in equation (3) extends over all I_k alternatives in subset K and J_k denotes the index of the first alternative in this subset.

The parameters θ_k, $K = 1 \ldots, K$ in Equations 2 and 3 are called the "dissimilarity parameters" of subset K. They are the essential parameters that provide the flexibility of the nested multinomial logit model. They characterize the differences between subsets and within subsets of the corrections among the ε_i (error terms). It becomes obvious from Equation 2 that the NMNL choice probabilities reduce to the MNL choice probabilities

$$P_i(V) = \frac{\exp(V_i)}{\sum_{j=1..I} \exp(V_j)}$$

if all θ_k equal unity. The difference of the dissimilarity coefficients from unity is a measure of the importance of similarities and dissimilarities among choices and a basis for specification tests. As for the role of the dissimilarity parameter, each θ_k not equal to one introduces a non-zero correlation among the disturbances ε_i within the subset K. Thus, it overcomes the assumption of "Independence of Irrelevant Alternatives" which is the major disadvantage of the MNL model.

It is also possible that groups of alternatives may themselves be more or less similar to each other. Thus, we can imagine more than two levels of nesting, hierarchically introducing similar and dissimilar alternatives on each level.

In considering hierarchical choice models of more than two levels it is useful to visualize them as defining a pattern of linkages among groups of similar alternatives. Each of the linkages corresponds to a choice among subsets of alternatives.

In the simple MNL model, (Fig. 3.1) all the elemental alternatives are linked directly, as in Fig. 3.1 (A). In a two-level nested choice model, some of the linkages lead to subset of alternatives rather than a single alternative as in Fig. 3.1 (B). There may also be a cluster of subsets of alternatives, as in Fig. 3.1 (C); thus establishing a hie-archy of similarities. Another way to look at it is in the form of a "decision tree." Figures 3.1 (A, B, and C) presents the "decision trees" corresponding to the cluster of similar alternatives. It should be pointed out that recursiveness is an important feature of such decision trees. It connects the levels with each other in a way that the attributes of all lower branch alternatives . . . contained in the inclusive value . . . influence the decision among any set of upper branches. That is, the higher level decisions are made in the light of the fact that the lower alternatives or clusters are already chosen as optimal in the respective lower subsets. This similarity is the fundamental differences of the nested logit model from a pure sequence of otherwise unrelated choice models. It has also been stated by McFadden that the hierarchy of choices and the notion of a "decision tree" are purely analytical devices; they do not imply that an individual necessarily follows a "path" down the tree, making choices in a certain order.

Sequential Estimation of NMNL Models

NMNL models can be estimated sequentially at any level of clustering. The sequential procedure starts with the MNL estimation of the lower level choice probabilities and the computation of the inclusive value at the lower level of the hierarchy, then it is carried out at each higher level. This approach has been applied to a large number of problems in transportation and urban economics (see Domencich and McFadden, 1975 and Anas, 1982). This method is computationally very convenient but suffers from two major disadvantages. Though consistent, the sequential estimator is inefficient, i.e., it produces high standard errors for a given sample information. This bias is particularly severe for complex decision trees. Furthermore, the sequential estimator cannot incorporate parameter restrictions across clusters and subgroups of alternatives.

CLUSTER OF SIMILR ALTERNATIVES

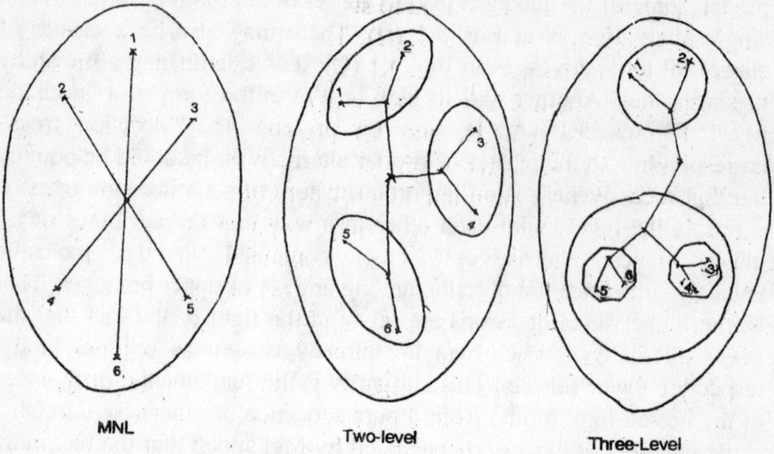

FIG. 3.1: Hierarchical Choice Models

The first disadvantage relates to the flow of information. The sequential estimator uses all the information of the lower branches to estimate the dissimilarity coefficients at the upper level, but not conversely. This leads to inefficiency. In addition, the standard errors of all the estimated coefficients in the upper levels have to be corrected for the presence of the lower level dissimilarity coefficients that have been estimated and are thus subject to randomness (Amemiya, 1978).

There are several versions of a hybrid between sequential estimation nd direct maximization. Small and Brownstone (1982) proposed a single full information maximum likelihood step starting from the sequential estimates. In theory, this yields asymptotically efficient estimates. In practice, this method faces several problems:

1. Consistency and asymptotic efficiency are properties of large samples.
2. The FIML likelihood function is highly nonlinear; and
3. Initial estimates of the sequential estimator are not likely to lie in a close neighborhood of the FIML estimates.

The combination of these factors implies that the one-step estimator tends to be close to the FIML estimates only when the dissimilarity coefficients are close to unity (Small and Brownstone, 1982).

The second disadvantage of the sequential estimation method (Fig. 3.2) is that if the alternatives in different clusters have common coefficients in their deterministic utility components, a proportionality constraint has to be fulfilled which destroys the sequential decomposition of the likelihood function. As an example, if we populate a two-level NMNL demand function that has tenure choice on the upper level (owning and renting) and size choice on the lower level of alternatives (size measured in number of rooms) we may hypothesize that the convenience of an additional room is weighted equally in the utility function of owners and renters. Similarly, we may think of a common price coefficient for all housing alternatives. Let γ denote such a parameter that is common across alternatives of different branches. In our example, the branches are characterized by the dissimilarity parameters θ_1 (for owners) and θ_2 (for renters).

The sequential estimator estimates separately the parameters of the lowest level $(\gamma/\theta)_1$ and $(\gamma/\theta)_2$ in the choice of dwelling size. Two MNL estimators are carried out, yielding the estimates $(\gamma/\theta)_1$ in the sample of owners and $(\gamma/\theta P)_{-2}$ in the sample of renters. Then, the inclusive values for owners and renters are computed. Finally, the binary choice between the two clusters identified, θ_1 and θ_2 at the second level. A common γ for owners and renters implies that:

$$\gamma = (\gamma/\theta)_1 . \theta_1 = (\gamma/\theta)_2 . \theta_2$$

However, the validity of Equation 4 is not guaranteed by the sequential estimation procedure.

Specification Tests

In specifying a nested multinomial logit model two important questions arise:

1. Is the difference between the simple MNL model and the nested MNL model significant; and
2. If the MNL model with its assumptions of independence of irrelevant alternatives (IIA) is rejected, what nesting structure is appropriate?

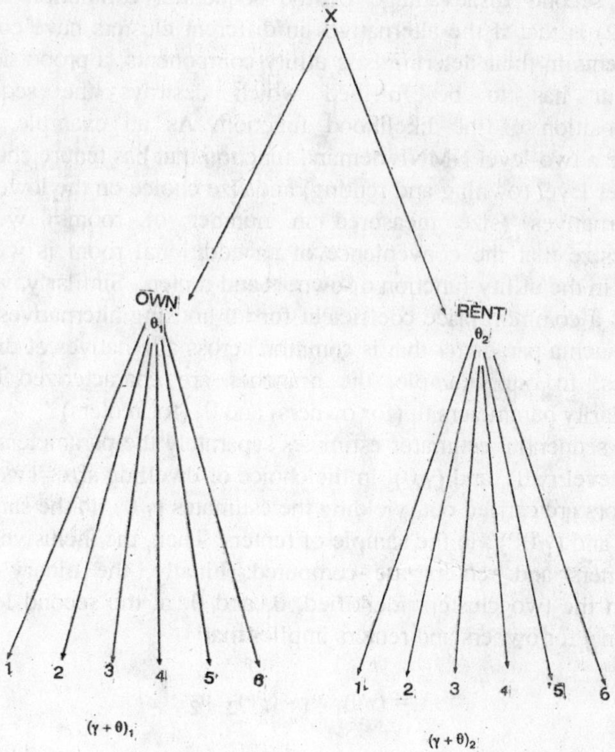

FIG. 3.2: Inter-cluster Constraints in NMML Models

Survey of Empirical Results

In this section of the survey of literature we focus on the empirical findings of the housing studies. We begin by identifying two broad bodies of literature. The review begins with studies relating to a micro-economic consumer theory of housing demand. Studies which have traditionally focused on estimating income and price elasticities of housing demand in both developed and developing countries. This exercise will be useful in comparing the elasticity results in this study. Then we look at some recent extensions of the micro-economic consumer theory to socio-demographic characteristics, limiting the review to housing choice studies.

The literature on housing demand indicates that there has been little agreement on what the income elasticities of demand are for housing. Historically, the major debate has focused on the Engle's law which asserts that the production of income spent on housing remains constant with rising income (Elasticity is unity), and Schwabe's law which asserts that the proportion decreases with increasing income. Studies since the early fifties have shown a wide range of income elasticities. Most cross-sectional investigations before 1955 are summed up by Houlkakker (1957) in a survey article of thirty-three countries. By means of a double-log Engel function he calculated a number of income elasticities. He found that the most of the elasticities were below unity. In a later study of thirteen OECD countries, Houlkakker's (1965) estimates ranged from 0.33 in Belgium to 1.99 in Norway.

Deleeuw (1971), in a cross-sectional evidence on the U.S. housing demand in the sixties, found that income elasticities estimates for housing ranged from 0.4 to 2.1. Muth's study (1960) of the demand for housing in U.S. cities included a cross-sectional analysis of the value per unit of detached single family homes in relation to family income, construction costs, and number of persons per household. His estimated income elasticity was 1.68.

In contrast to Muth, Lee's cross-sectional study (1968) which was based on individual spending unit re-interviewed over a three-year period by the Survey Research Centre at the University of Michigan. Data on income and rental expenditures and housing values were included in the survey. Lee made use of the instrumental variable technique to relate housing to income for more than one year. His income elasticity estimates were very low; 0.65 for renters households, and 0.80 for owners. Winger (1968), in another study found an income elasticity estimates of about 1.05 for all housing units.

The findings of these studies have left some questions unanswered. For instance, one is not exactly sure whether the variation in income elasticities were attributable to peculiarities in the database, to the definition of variables, or to the inherent biases in the use of micro-data. Further these studies did not exactly explain why owner and renter elasticities differed so markedly. Some current studies have tried to answer the questions left open by earlier studies. Nelson (1975), for example estimated demand equations based on individual household observations. When the same observations were grouped by census tract, the income elasticity estimates rose from 0.28 and 0.24 to 0.76 and 1.16 respectively for renters and owners. Nelson also made an attempt to use aggregate data with grouping procedures less prone to aggregation bias (by grouping randomly and by income class) and found that the micro estimates and grouped estimates were quite close together. His estimates changed from 0.28 to 0.35 for renters and 0.24 to 0.36 for owners.

Most studies on housing demand relegate price elasticity to a somewhat of a secondary level of analysis. Such estimates have been shown to be sensitive to, in which prices are defined and to the model specification. Analysis Using BLS data have indicated price elasticities from about –0.3 to –0.9 for owners (Maisel, Burnham, and Austin, 1971). Muth (1974) obtained an estimate of –0.76, Polinsky and Elwood –0.67, and Rosen an estimate of –0.67. Despite these variations in price estimates, most studies indicate that the demand for housing is price inelastic.

When we turn to studies in developing countries relatively little work has been done on housing demand using micro level data, partly because of data constraints and partly because only in the past decade have urbanization and its attendant problems become a major policy issue. Studies have been recently conducted in Korea, Columbia, and El Salvador under the direction of the World Bank (Ingram, 1981; Follain, 1980; Strassman, 1980; and Jinenez and Keare, 1984). An interesting result of these studies is that the magnitude of these estimates of income elasticities are remarkably similar to those found in developed countries. Follain (1980) found income elasticity of 0.6 for owners and 0.4 for renters in Korea. Under normal circumstances, the use of current income to estimate income elasticities of demand would lead to estimates which would be biased downwards in proportion to the ratio of variance in permanent income. Therefore one would expect this bias to be particularly severe in developing countries where, with a large urban informal sector, the transitory income component could have a large variance because of irregular employment and earnings. Mishkin (1976), however, has argued that the permanent income hypothesis may not hold in the absence of well functioning capital markets in developing countries. This hypothesis is supported by the study of Jimenez and Kaere (1984) which found permanent income elasticity of housing demand in El Salvador to be only slightly larger than the current income elasticity. This implies that using current income for demand estimation in developing countries may be sufficient to give us close estimates which are not misleading.

Aside from studies connected strictly with estimating income and price elasticities, there are also studies that provide evidence that the demand for housing varies with the level of economic development and the level of urbanization in a country. Lakshmanan, Chatterjee, and Knoll's study (1978) supports the hypothesis that income elasticities of demand are low in the early stages of development, when a Nations resources are directed to other productive sectors, and increases rapidly in the middle stages of development as the housing sector catches up. Finally at high levels of development, housing demand again declines in relative terms as resources shift elsewhere.

The second body of literature in existence are those concerned with housing choice studies. These studies focus on the decision-making process of households. One study that follows the random utility theory approach was conducted by Alex Borsch-Supan (1985). This study brings out the differences in the housing choice decision of households in West Germany and the United States. The model used was a nested multinomial logit. The study found striking difference in the price elasticities between the countries. The magnitude of the price elasticities in Germany are larger for owners, but smaller for renters than in the United States. They study also points out that in Germany, a cost increase in ownership implies substitution into the rental market segment. In contrast substitution occur within the owner market in the United States. In Germany, a one per cent increase in out-of-pocket cost of single family owner occupied homes implies not only a reduction of 6.8 per cent in the market share of that alternative, but also a reduction of 5.1 per cent in the share of home ownership of large single family dwellings. The study concluded that Americans have a stronger tendency to stay in owner occupied housing than Germans do. The Germans are more price responsive as home owners and the Americans as renters. Tenure choice is also differently perceived in Germany than in the United States, where more income always implies a higher tendency to own. The main conclusion of the study may be summarized by the catchword "The American Dream"; Americans have a strong preference for large single family homes, even after statistical corrections for massive tax advantage of home ownership are made. Germans do not share this dream to this extent: they prefer owning to renting, but they considered large rental units attractive as well. Americans are highly responsive to price changes in the rental housing, much less so in owner-occupied housing. Germans exhibit a reverse pattern: their price elasticity of choosing owner occupied housing exceeds the corresponding elasticity to rent housing units. In Germany, price changes in one tenure category will unambiguously induce a shift in the tenure choice balance, whereas Americans are found to stay with home ownership even at increasing costs. Finally it is found that housing consumption is a much more important indicator for income class affiliation in the United States than it is in West Germany.

The overall performance of the model was found to be good, however the predictions are more precise in the American sample: the largest fraction of correctly predicted household is 78.4 per cent in the American sample, only 68.5 per cent in the German sample. Similar results were found by Williams (1979) who used a logit model virtually identical to that used in Quigley (1976) to estimate demand for neighborhood among households in Pittsburgh. Recent studies (Straszheim, 1973), which utilize data on individual households attempt to incorporate the multidimensional nature of housing which was largely ignored by previous studies. Williams's model predicts that the probability of a household choosing a home in a good neighborhood is higher if the household is larger, although seemingly random variations did occur within the coefficients. He also found out that large households tend to choose units with more bedrooms and higher income households are slightly more likely to reside in single family homes than their lower income counterparts. Large households are more likely to reside in single family structures, and large-lot units are more common among larger households. Smaller households, by contrast, are more likely to reside in multifamily structures. These results support those of Lerman (1979) and Segal (1979).

In study of private rental housing (Awam, Odlingsmec, and Whitehead) found that household characteristics affect the demand for private rental accommodations. Their results strongly support the conclusion that household of demand for housing as a whole was estimated to be low, but that for certain attributes, especially the quality of the dwelling high. Their results suggest that, space is by far the most important variable determining utility and that it is a necessary attribute. The study also found racial composition of the person to be an important determinant of housing choice. This result supports Quigley's findings. Quigley also provided evidence that dwelling condition, size, age and rent have an impact on the probability of housing choice. The importance of household characteristics has also been suggested by Ioannides (1987). He found that renter and owning price variables are highly significant for both renters and owners. He also found that higher income, age, family, size and white head of household all increase the likelihood of owning.

NOTES

1. Van Lierop, Wal., *Spatial Interaction Modeling and Residential Choice,* p. 122.
2. It is interesting to note that Lancaster's Multi-Attribute Theory of Consumer Behaviour dates back to similar ideas already put forward by Mengar in 1871.
3. This overview is partly based on Van Lierop and Nijkamp, 1982. For more details see among others: McFadden, 1978 and 1984; Williams and Ortuzar, 1982; Maddala, 1983 and Pitfield, 1984.
4. These approaches are traditionally applied more often to macro situations.
5. Hensher and Johnson (1981, PP. 105), write the following: "Independence indicates that the correlation between the unobserved attributes associated with each and every pair of alternatives in a choice set and across choice set is zero. Identically distributed means that taste variations exist over the observed attributes. Yet, it is neutral between alternatives, having the same distribution around the mean utility level."
6. Complete derivation of the multinomial logit formula is provided in McFadden, 1973.
7. The model or its variants could be derived in a number of ways. Its original formulation is due to Luce (1959).
8. See Luce and Suppes (1965).
9. The measurement in this respect might take place directly or indirectly by means of perception or even preference weights, which are transformed into cardinal values.
10. See Domencich and McFadden (1975).
11. It is evident that in the EBA model tradeoffs are not recognized.
12. See McFadden (1978).
13. The hierarchical elimination method assumes a hierarchy in the choice process. It always beings at the root of the tree and then selects in successive steps the relevant branches via the related aspects. Thus, in the estimation phase the method starts at the level of realized alternative choices and works back, step by step, until the most elementary aspect choice level is reached i.e., at the root of the tree. A general limitation of the hierarchical approaches is that the analyst must know the correct decision hierarchy beforehand. Without this knowledge, he has to experiment with models by trial and error.
14. "Econometric Analysis of Discrete Choice with Applications on the Demand for Housing in the U.S.A. and West Germany," published by Springer-Verlag, (1987).

4

RIO DE JANEIRO: A General Overview

Background

The State of Rio de Janeiro, located in the Southeast region of Brazil, was created by the fusion of two states (the ex-state of Guanabara and the old state of Rio in July 1974). It was formally installed as the new state of Rio in May, 1975.[1] According to Vetter and Brasileiro (1978),[2] this merger permitted the application of Law 14 which, in turn, created the new metropolitan region of Rio. Due to the region's initial growth and the accompanying circular and cumulative effects, the scope of urban problems in Rio began to expand beyond the spatial limits of the Municipios which were normally responsible for dealing with such problems. The revised Constitution of 1967 officially acknowledged the attendant problems associated with metropolitan growth and laid the groundwork for the establishment of metropolitan regions.

The Foundation for the Development of Rio de Janeiro (FUNDERM), with its own criteria for delimitation purposes, identifies five administrative regions in the state of Rio. They are the metropolitan region itself, the hilly region of the Mar escarpment bordering the metropolitan region, the Sun coast region located east of the metro area, the Green coast region located west of the metro area, and finally the Northern region.

The City of Rio de Janeiro served as the capital of Brazil from 1763, when the seat was transferred from Salvador, Bahia until 1960, when the capital was transferred to Brasilia. The two hundred-year history as a capital city propelled Rio into economic and political dominance and accounted for its cosmopolitan nature. Besides the regional division outlined by the Foundation for the Development of Rio de Janeiro, a number of other regional delimitations exists for the State of Rio. The Brazilian Institute for Geography and Statistics divides the State of Rio into fourteen homogeneous regions as indicated in Fig. 4.2. The purpose of this division was to provide a regional division of the State into areas as homogeneous as possible, with respect to physical, social, and economic characteristics.

The Brazilian Institute for Geography and Statistics (IBGE) also recognizes three broad regions in the State of Rio. These are the outer Peripheral Region, the greater Rio Region, and the municipality of Rio de Janeiro, which is the focus of this study. The outer Peripheral Region consists of those regions lying beyond the limits of metropolitan region of Rio. Collectively the region accounts for approximately 23 per cent of the State of Rio's population. There are some light industries in some of the urban areas in this region; however, tourism seems to be an important activity in the outer Peripheral Region. These activities are supplemented by dairying and mixed agricultural activities.

The other two regions fall within the boundary of Rio Metropolitan Area (RMA). The Metropolitan Region of Rio had a population of approximately 9,153,156 in 1980 (see Table 4.1). This accounted for 79.1 per cent of the State of Rio's population. The City of Rio's population growth rate relative to other municipalities has slowed down over the past decade. Although the city accounted for the highest share of the State's population (45.1%) and the Metropolitan Region's population (56.6%) in 1980, higher population growth rates in 1970 and 1980 were recorded in other regions like Greater Rio (Table 4.1). The unexpected growth of population in Greater Rio is a reflection of the urbanization process resulting from the effects of the City of Rio and the influx of migrants from the bordering states, making it one of the most crowded cities of the world.

The municipality of Rio which is the focus of the study is often assumed to be a homogeneous entity. It is completely urbanized (100% urban) and enjoys a relatively high standard of living; however this assumption seems to be misleading because our analysis indicates socio-economic disparities do exist in the municipality of Rio (Table 4.2). In order to highlight the existing disparities we computed the per capita household income of the residents of the Rio municipality. The municipality of Rio consists of eleven different localities. Santa Cruz has a mean per capita monthly income of only 3,094 cruzeiros and Botafago has a mean per capita monthly income of 24,386 cruzeiros (Table 4.2). In a study of housing choice it is important that such disparities should be taken into consideration in order to reduce the aggregation problems that may arise from an erroneous assumption of homogeneity.

TABLE 4.1: Demographic Characteristics of Micro-regions in the States of Rio, 1980

Micro Regions	Total Population	Per cent Population	Per cent Urban	Per cent Growth (1970-80)
State of Rio	11,449,767	100.0	91.7	20.3
Itaperuna	134,478	1.2	56.8	1.0
Miracema	77,459	0.7	56.7	0.1
Acurcareira de Campos	536,912	4.7	58.2	9.5
Cantagerlo	73,972	0.6	39.6	2.5
Tres Rio	116,971	1.0	76.5	17.5
Corderiro	65,323	0.5	43.4	-1.2
Vale do Paraiba	582,085	5.1	86.9	40.6
Serrana Fluminese	473,576	4.1	84.9	31.9
Vassouras Epivai	132,262	1.2	58.9	10.3
Bacais do Sao	116,706	1.0	52.2	—
Cabo Frio	189,566	1.6	74.1	37.8
Bai Ilha Grande	84,723	0.7	45.4	32.9
Greater Rio	3,721,652	32.4	95.8	39.6
City of Rio	5,183,992	45.1	100.0	20.1
Petropolis	247,512	2.2	98.5	31.9
*Rio Metro-Politan	9,153,156	79.7	98.5	28.5

* Includes Cites of Rio, Greater Rio, and Petropolis.

TABLE 4.2: Administrative Regions in City of Rio De Janeiro

Administrative Regions	Principle Sample	Per Capita Household Income	Mean Rent
Protuaria/Sao Cristaro	111	7,514	1,372
Central Santa Teresa	152	12,921	3,139
Isabel	966	16,728	4,041
Botafago	875	24,386	5,734
Lagoa	721	20,605	6,402
Ramos	280	7,987	2,070
Penha	352	8,077	1,837
Meier	850	8,023	2,032
Iraja	1,615	6,406	1,535
Santo Cruz	103	3,094	458
Ilha	178	9,575	2,516
Total	6,203	12,803	2,138

In order to highlight the intra-urban income disparities that exist in Rio, we have divided the municipality into three regions: Low Income Region, Middle Income Region, and High Income Region. These sub-divisions are based on the mean monthly per capita household income. Per capita household income was computed by dividing total household income from all sources by the household size. According to Musgrave (1978),[3] the variation in the household size is much too great in Rio to be ignored. Three different criteria were used to group the eleven administrative areas in Rio municipality into Low Income, Middle Income, and High Income regions. We conducted an *F*-Test on all the areas in Rio which gave us an *F*-value of 89.6. This suggests that there is a significant difference in the mean per capita income of household between the eléven administrative areas. In order to be able to condense the eleven administrative areas into three regions we grouped all the areas into three groups: Low Income, Middle Income, and High Income, and conducted an analysis of variance for each of these three groups. The results of the test are presented in Table 4.3. The *F*-value for the first group was 1.96. This suggests that there is no significant difference at both the 95 per cent and 99 per cent levels in per capita mean household income between the three administrative areas of Postuaria, Iraja, and Santa Cruz. For the other two groups the *F*-value was 4.96 and 3.9 respectively, which suggests that there is a significant difference between the mean per capita income of the areas within the two groups. Several other groupings of eleven administrative areas were attempted. However, the *F*-value for any other classification into groups were much higher. The *F*-values reported in the table are the lowest values. In order to justify our grouping we further conducted a range test. This test produces two types of outputs. The first type of output is a multiple comparison between all groups where non-empty group means are sorted in ascending order. An asterisk in the matrix indicates significantly different group means. In addition the range test produces homogeneous subsets. Areas will be placed in a subset if the highest and lowest means do not differ by more than the shortest significant range for a subset of that size. The subsets derived from the range test are consistent with the grouping indicated based on the *F*-test.

The third criterion used to group administrative areas is the one used by the Brazilian Government. Minimum salary and poverty levels were used as cut-offs for delimiting the respective regions. Vetter (1982)[4] mentions that the minimum salary for Brazil in November

1980 was 5,789 cruzeiros. Barbosa (1985)[5] indicates that the National Bank for Housing (B.N.H.) established three minimum salaries as the poverty level for 1980; therefore this study has distinguished areas which have household incomes less than or equal to three minimum salaries as low income regions, areas between four to six minimum salaries are classified as middle income, and regions with those with seven or more minimum salaries were designated as high income regions. The grouping of administrative areas based on the minimum salary poverty line closely conform with the groupings based on the F-test and the range test discussed earlier.

TABLE 4.3: Analysis of Variance Test Results

Group	Administrative Regions	Per Capita Household Income	F-value
Low Income Region	Protuaria	7,514	
	Iraja	6,406	1.96
	Santa Cruz	3,094	
Middle Income Region	Centro	12,921	
	Isabel	16,728	
	Ramos	7,987	4.96
	Penha	8,077	
	Meier	8,023	
	Ilha	9,575	
High Income Region	Lagoa	20,605	3.9
	Botafago	24,386	

Observe an interesting pattern of settlement by looking at the map (Fig. 4.1). First of all, the three regions form contiguous zones thereby fulfilling an important criterion mentioned by Goodman[6] for classifying housing submarkets. The upper income Southern coastal zone extends from the Southwestern portions of Guanbana Bay through the prosperous narrow strip of beach front development in Botafago. Griffin and Ford[7] describe how this sector is characterized almost exclusively by modern high-rise apartments and hotels. This region underwent a massive slum (Favela) eradication between 1968 and 1972. Portes[8] states that during this period 9,789 favelas, forming 59 per cent of all favelas were removed from this region alone. The purpose of favela eradication was to free up land for the construction of upper income and commercial residences as well as industrial parks as a part of the "industrial growth pole" strategy. This region has the

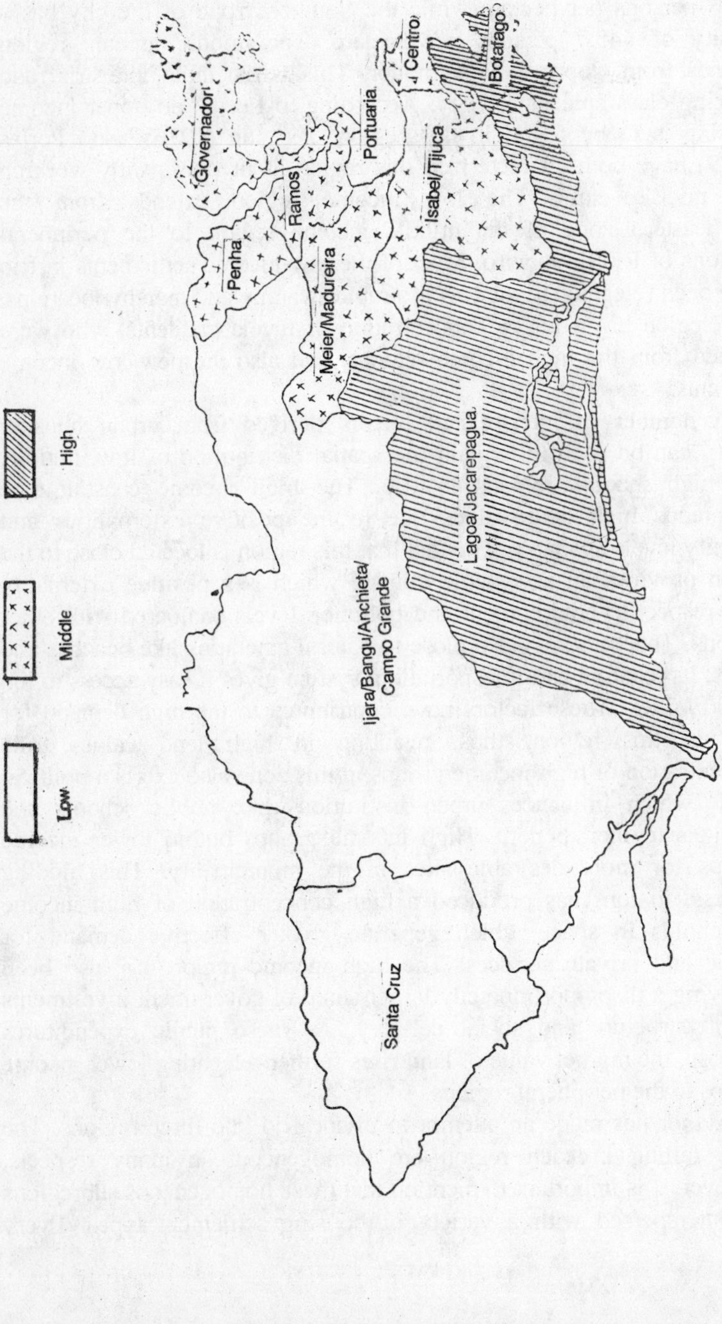

FIG. 4.1: Rop de Janeiro: Low, Middle and High Income Regions

highest urban density in Rio. The City of Rio has an average density of 122.6 persons per hectare while the Southern zone of the city has a density of 445.7 persons per hectare. The middle income region extends from Cupro to Governador. This is the main industrial and working class area of the city. According to Leeds[9] no upper income housing is to be found in this region. Perlman (1976)[10] and Portes (1979) have both characterized this region as predominantly working and middle class. The low income region extends from the Northeastern zone of the middle income region to the peripheral portions of Rio de Janeiro. Most of the low income settlements in Rio have been relegated to the less desirable swampy and marshy locations. This region has a heavy concentration of favela residents, who were evicted from the high income regions, and also the new low income migrants.

A number of inter-related factors derived from urban housing theory can be used to explain the spatial distribution of low, middle, and high income regions in Rio. The high income coastal zone commands high land values due to the positive externalities and amenity levels available. The fact that this region is located close to the ocean provides an acceptable climate which is a positive externality with respect to environment and pollution levels compared with other regions. This region is also close to natural amenities like beaches and parks. Its location and transportation system gives it easy access to job opportunities. These factors have contributed to the high demand for land in this region, thus, resulting in high land values. The concentration of high income groups in this zone also exerts a political "pull" which influences urban institutions like public schools and hospitals to their benefit. High income groups outbid lower income groups for more desirable sites in the municipality. This bidding process, in turn has produced a high concentration of high income households in space which generate greater effective demand for public and private services. The high income region has also been receiving a disproportionatelly larger share of government investments in infrastructure and social delivery. As these public expenditures increase, the market value of land rises further relegating lower income groups to the peripheral regions.

Author has made an attempt to divide Rio into three regions. The areas falling in each region are homogeneous in many respects, however, it is important to mention that these homogeneous subregions are interspersed with a variety of housing settlement types. Every region has a number of different types of housing to choose from, a fact which is discussed in more detail in the next section of this chapter.

Dwelling Condition and Household Attributes

There is currently little systematic work on housing submarkets and housing attributes in developing countries. Most work is at the case study level and is based on field experience (Leeds, 1974; Peattie, 1974 and Perlman, 1976). In this section the housing consumption package in Rio is assessed with respect to durability of housing units (structural characteristics); public service delivery system (amenity/infrastructure levels); and the size and space dimensions of units (number of rooms). Housing quality in Rio is determined by a set of attributes as measured by the physical characteristics of the units and the levels of infrastructure services it receives.

The first part of this section focuses on intra-urban variations in the quality of the housing stock in urban Rio. Housing stock refers to physical facilities and is usually differentiated from that of housing services. The second half of this section deals with an examination of the composition of households in Rio with respect to such socio-demographic attributes such as household size, age, education, and occupation of household heads.

Housing Stock Attributes

The structural characteristics of a dwelling unit is determined by the type of material used in its construction. It is an important consideration in classifying housing into different types. This classification will enter into the housing choice model. Table 4.4 lists the different types of durable and non-durable materials used in the construction of dwelling units in Rio. A quick glance at the table indicates that a large proportion of dwelling units have walls, roofs, and floors constructed with durable materials. 94.7 per cent of all dwelling units have walls constructed with brick or stone, which are highly durable materials which increase the life of the house. It is evident from Table 4.4 that wood floors appear to be a superior good. 68.6 per cent of the dwellings have wood floors, 24.6 per cent of all dwelling units have cement floors; they appear to be inferior goods. (This is because they tend to be mixed with a considerable amount of sand and soil). When a comparison is made between the three regions we came up with come interesting results. A large proportion of dwellings in the low income, middle income, and high income regions use brick and stone in wall construction (95.8, 93.4, and 95.7% respectively). however, the same cannot be said regarding floors and roofs. As we move from low income regions to the high income regions we find that a larger and larger proportion of dwelling units have floors and roofs made of durable materials (wood, timber): Only 45.7 per cent of all dwelling units in the low income region have wooden floors, 73.1 per cent in the middle income region and 87.0 per cent in the high income region. Only 33.6 per cent of dwelling units in the low income regions have roofs made from concrete slabs (the most durable material), compared to 55.2 per cent in the middle income region and 81.7 per cent in the high income region. This seems to suggest why housing prices would tend to rise as we move from low income to high income regions. It should also be pointed out that housing is a move superior good and therefore, as expected, the structural quality of dwelling units improve systematically from the low income region to the high income region. The data in Table 4.4 are aggregate estimates which fail to highlight the variation in housing stock by housing type. A comparison of Tables 4.5 and 4.6 provide some valuable insights pertaining to such variation. It is evident that apartments in general have durable material used in construction of walls, floors, and roofs compared with the houses irrespective of whether they are located in low, middle, or high income regions. This should not be surprising since most apartments are in the high income region which are considered to be luxury high rise duplexes that border the coastal strip. Table 4.5 summarizes information on the structural condition of houses. Again, strictly from the point of view of data presented, this housing category enjoys the comforts associated with durable housing, but not as much as apartment dwellers. A high proportion of houses in Rio have durable walls and floors. Most, however, are covered by clay tiles especially those in the low income region (54.1%).

The tables also suggest that there are variations in housing quality as far as materials are concerned between regions in the cases of houses. As we move from a low income region to a high income region more durable materials have been used in the construction of houses.

TABLE 4.4: Stock and Infrastructural Characteristics of Dwelling Units in the City of Rio De Janeiro

Indicators	Urban Rio	Low Income Region	Mid Income Region	High Income Region
Sample Size	6,023	1,829	2,778	1,596
Walls				
Brick/Stone	94.7	95.8	93.4	95.7
Timber	2.8	3.2	3.1	2.1
Clay/Plaster	1.1	0.2	1.6	1.1
Recycled Material	.001	0.2	1.3	0.2
Floors				
Timber	68.6	45.7	73.1	87.0
Cement	24.6	43.5	20.9,	9.3
Clay	4.8	8.8	3.7	2.0
Recycled Materiel	0.24	0.2	0.4	0.1
Roof				
Concrete Slab	55.7	33.6	55.2	81.7
Cement	8.8	15.9	4.3	3.6
Clay Tiles	33.8	48.7	36.0	13.2

TABLE 4.5: Stock and Infrastructural Characteristics of Houses by Region in the City of Rio De Janeiro

Indicators	Urban Rio	Low Income Region	Mid Income Region	High Income Region
Sample Size	3,525	1,557	1,606	362
Walls				
Brick/Stone	92.0	95.6	89.9	86.5
Timber	4.8	3.8	5.2	7.2
Clay/Plaster	1.9	0.3	2.7	5.0
Recycled Material	1.2	0.3	2.2	0.8
Floors				
Timber	50.3	39.9	58.0	60.8
Cement	41.2	50.0	34.4	33.1
Clay	6.4	8.6	4.9	3.6
Recycled Material	0.4	0.2	0.7	0.3
Roof				
Concrete Slab	30.9	27.1	33.1	37.0
Cement	11.5	17.3	5.8	11.6
Clay Tiles	53.8	54.1	54.7	48.3

TABLE 4.6: Stock and Infrastructural Characteristics of Apartments by Region in the City of Rio De Janeiro

Indicators	Urban Rio	Low Income Region	Mid Income Region	High Income Region
Sample Size	2,642	263	1,156	1,223
Walls				
Brick/Stone	99.6	100.0	99.7	99.3
Timber	0.4	0.0	0.2	0.6
Clay/Plaster	0.0	0.0	0.0	0.0
Recycled Material	0.0	0.0	0.0	0.0
Floors				
Timber	94.0	81.7	95.1	95.6
Cement	2.8	6.8	2.4	2.3
Clay	2.6	10.3	2.1	1.6
Recycled Material	0.0	0.0	0.0	0.0
Roof				
Concrete Slab	89.5	93.4	86.6	95.7
Cement	2.4	8.0	2.2	1.3
Clay Tiles	7.8	18.6	10.4	2.9

Dwelling Unit Size in Rio

Table 4.7 summarizes information on the size of the dwelling units in Rio as measured by the number of rooms and the number of bedrooms. It would be best to measure the size of the dwelling unit in terms of lot size and floor space available, but the data are not available. Given this fact, the number of rooms and bedrooms is used as a proxy for measuring the size of the unit. This type of a measure was used by Axel Borsch Supan[11] in his study of housing choice in the United States and West Germany.

In the City of Rio overall there seems to be a positive relationship between the number of rooms and the regions in which the dwelling units are located. In the case of houses only 12.6 per cent of the units located in the low income region have seven or more rooms compared to 17.6 per cent in the middle income region and 20.4 per cent in the high income region. The differences are much more pronounced in the case of apartment units, with 22.1 per cent of the apartments in the low income region having seven or more rooms compared with 38.8 per cent in the middle income region and 50.9 per cent in the high income region. Given these trends we would expect apartment complexes to be associated with lower densities. (Housing density is measured by the number of people per room). A similar trend exists in the number of bedrooms between houses and apartments in the three regions. The number of bedrooms increases both among houses and apartments as

TABLE 4.7: Room Capacity by Housing Type and Region in Urban Rio

	Low Income Regions	Mid Income Regions	High Income Regions
Houses			
Number of Rooms			
1-2	11.9	13.9	12.7
3-4	37.1	34.7	32.3
5-6	38.4	33.7	34.5
7+	12.6	17.6	20.4
Number of Bedrooms			
1-2	83.2	80.6	79.0
3-4	16.4	18.2	18.2
5+	0.4	1.2	2.8
Apartments			
Number of Rooms			
1-2	7.6	4.1	5.1
3-4	12.5	17.6	21.1
5-6	57.8	39.6	22.9
7+	22.1	38.8	50.9
Number Of Bedrooms			
1-2	80.2	76.3	67.6
3-4	19.6	23.4	31.1
5+	0.0	0.3	1.3

we move from low income regions to high income regions. If we compare Table 4.8 with Table 4.6 some insights can be gained on the housing density. We find that the size of the house per person increases consistently with region. With lower income regions accounting for larger household size and high incomes having smaller household size, this indicates that the number of persons per room would be greater in low income regions compared to the other two regions. This seems to confirm the long standing belief that low income households tend to have larger families compared to the high income households.

TABLE 4.8: Socio-demographic Characteristics of Households by Housing Type and by Region in Rio

Age of Head	Urban Rio	Low Income Region	Mid Income Region	High Income Region
Houses				
< 24	5.5	5.4	5.4	6.9
25 - 34	23.8	25.4	22.8	22.1
35 - 44	22.8	25.3	21.0	20.2
45 - 54	20.8	22.0	20.0	20.7
55 - 64	14.0	12.1	16.7	13.8
Over 65	13.7	9.8	14.1	16.3
Apartments				
< 24	21.4	3.4	3.0	3.2
25 - 34	22.1	30.0	21.3	21.2
35 - 44	23.7	26.2	24.2	22.6
45 - 54	21.7	16.7	22.9	21.7
55 - 64	16.3	13.7	17.0	16.4
Over 65	12.9	9.9	11.5	14.9

Household Characteristics

A detailed study of housing choice behaviour not only involves an analysis of the type of housing being chosen but also the essential attributes of the households who make these choices, so as to incorporate taste variations in the decision process. In this section a description of some of the important characteristics which are expected have an impact on the tastes of household in making a housing choice are presented.

Age Composition

Rio has a typical age composition. The majority of the household heads are in the intermediate age group, that is between the ages of 35 and 54, with relatively fewer younger and older household heads. This pattern is prevalent in the different regions of Rio.

Table 4.8 shows the age composition of household heads by housing type and by region. It allows us in this case to detect whether age composition has an impact on the household head's choice of housing and location. Younger household heads opt more frequently for houses rather than apartments. A possible explanation for this trend is that houses are more affordable than the high quality duplexes or apartments. The table also suggests that older household heads prefer apartments over houses; and more of them prefer to locate in the high income region. We would expect this trend because older household heads may have higher incomes and also the possibility that there may be more than one household member working, thus, making it possible to choose luxury apartments complexes.

Size of Household

Table 4.9 reveals that 35.9 per cent of the small households (1-2 members) opt for an apartment compared with only 24.4 per cent opting for houses, however, for other family sizes there is no differential pattern. The table indicates that almost an equal proportion of small, intermediate, and large households are distributed evenly among houses and apartment units suggesting no correlation between household size and the choice of dwelling type. A slight variation exists in the 1-2 member households between the regions. Overall, the majority of the household in Rio and its regions are small to medium sized households not exceeding six members. There are also indications that in general low income households out-number high income households in the larger size categories. Larger size households living in high income regions tend to opt for their own houses over apartment units.

Education of Household Head

Table 4.10 indicates that for urban Rio as a whole the majority of households have completed at least the primary level of education (3-4 years). Intra-urban variations in educational levels reveal the expected pattern with upper income regions accounts for the highest education levels. Disaggregation by housing type provides some interesting patterns. Household heads who have at least entered high school education (9 to 11 years) of education opt for more expensive, high quality complexes. We also notice that only 6.2 per cent of all heads who have twelve or more years of schooling opt for houses compared with 31.2 per cent who opt for apartments. A larger proportion of households living in apartments having a low education level live in the low income regions compared with those with higher education levels. There seems to be a substantial intra-urban variation in housing choice among households with different educational levels. The table also reveals that households in low income regions with high educational levels prefer high-quality complexes. Musgrave (1978) has discussed the variations in household tastes and educational levels of households. The preference structure of highly-educated low income household heads for luxury apartments could be a reflection of the higher tastes that they have acquired, tastes which they may prefer to satisfy irrespective of their incomes. On the other hand, low income household heads with fewer years of schooling (0-2) opt for more affordable houses.

TABLE 4.9: Size of Household by Housing Type and by Region in Rio, 1980

Size of Household	Urban Rio	Low Income Region	Mid Income Region	High Income Region
Houses				
1-2	24.2	21.9	26.7	25.4
3-4	41.3	41.2	41.6	40.9
5-6	23.0	25.1	20.9	23.5
7-8	7.3	7.9	6.8	6.9
Over 9	3.8	3.9	3.9	3.3
Apartments				
1-2	35.9	28.5	33.8	39.6
3-4	40.8	45.6	42.6	38.2
5-6	18.8	19.0	19.6	18.2
7-8	3.6	4.9	3.5	3.5
Over 9	0.7	1.9	0.5	0.6

TABLE 4.10: Education of Head of Household by Housing Type and by Region for Urban Rio, 1980

Education of Head	Urban Rio	Low Income Region	Mid Income Region	High Income Region
Houses				
0	12.0	10.1	13.1	15.7
1-2	8.2	8.3	7.7	10.7
3-4 (primary)	41.5	45.9	40.2	31.8
4-8 (middle	21.2	22.5	20.2	21.0
9-11 (high)	10.4	10.0	11.1	9.1
12+	6.2	3.9	7.6	10.2
Apartments				
0	2.6	4.9	2.2	2.6
1-2	2.11	2.3	2.9	2.0
3-4 (primary)	19.6	28.9	23.4	14.1
4-8 (middle)	21.6	24.7	22.5	20.0
9-11 (high)	21.6	24.3	22.8	20.0
12+	31.2	14.4	26.2	39.6

Occupation of Household Head

The occupational distribution of household heads in Rio is presented in Table 4.11. Over 50 per cent of the household heads are employed in administrative, professional, and manufacturing- and construction-related occupations. Since Rio is 100 per cent urbanized, as would be expected agriculture and mining accounts for the lowest employment category. Twelve per cent of the households are employed in service industry-related occupations. For the administrative and professional groups, the intra-income region variations are substantial. A larger proportion of household heads residing in the high income group region belong to the Administrative and Professional occupations. We would expect education, income, and occupation to be correlated. The low income region has a higher concentration in the manufacturing and construction sector; these are household heads in general with low educational levels. It should also be pointed out that the majority of jobs in manufacturing and construction require physical labor. Thus, there is a tendency for the low income region to have higher concentrations of less educated households. The table also indicates that the middle income region has the largest share of household heads in trade-related occupations.

TABLE 4.11: Occupation of Head of the Household by Region in Rio, 1980

Occupation of Head	Urban Rio	Low Income Region	Mid Income Region	High Income Region
Administrative	17.9	16.5	23.1	29.2
Professional	14.3	5.5	12.8	26.7
Agriculture & Mining	0.7	1.8	0.2	0.3
Manufacturing & Construction	20.0	27.2	21.0	10.5
Trade	9.5	9.3	10.7	7.6
Transportation & Communication	8.2	11.1	7.8	5.7
Service	12.0	12.4	11.8	11.8
Defense	5.3	8.0	5.4	2.2
Other	7.0	8.0	7.1	6.1

NOTES

1. The formation of a new metropolitan region within the state was necessitated by the inadequacy of existing legal institutions for dealing with metropolitan problems.
2. Veter, D.M. and Brasileiro, A.M. (1978). "Towards a Development Strategy for Grande Rio de Janeiro." *Latin America Urban Research*, 6, pp.259-279.
3. Musgrave, P. 1978. *Consumer Behavior in Latin America.* Brookings Institute, Washington, D.C.
4. Vetter, D.M. 1982. "Per Capita Family Income as a Measure of Family Income and Its Variations Over the Family Life Cycle" (Mimeograph), IBGE, Brazil.
5. Barbosa, E. 1985. "Housing The Urban Poor in Rio de Janeiro." Unpublished Ph.D Dissertation, Boston University, Boston, Massachusetts.
6. Goodman, J. 1976. "Housing Consumption, Disequilibrium, and Local Residential Mobility." *Environment and Planning*, 8, pp. 855-875.
7. Griffin, E. and L. Ford. 1983. "Cities of Latin America." in *Cities of the World: World Regional Urban Development*, pp.197-237. Harper and Row Publishing Company, New York.
8. Portes, A. 1979. "Housing Policy, Urban Poverty, and the State: The Favelas of Rio de Janeiro: 1976." *Latin America Research Review*, Volume 14, number 2, pp. 3-24.
9. Leeds, A. 1974. "Housing Settlement Types, Arrangements for Living, Proletarianization, and the Social Structure of the City" in *Anthropological Perspectives on Latin American Urbanization: Latin American Urban Research*, Volume 4, Sage Publishing Company. Beverly Hills, California.
10. Perlman, J.E. 1976. "The Myth of Marginality: Urban Poverty and Politics in Rio de Janeiro," University of California Press, Berkley, California.
11. Borsch-Supan, Axel (1987). In his study he estimated the demand for housing in the U.S. and West Germany and indicated that the number of rooms is a good measure of housing size if information on lot size and floor space is not available.

5

LOGIT MODEL, VARIABLE SPECIFICATION AND DATABASE

The Model

The model estimated in this study is based on the utility approach of consumer theory. This approach with a random specification, has two major advantages: (1) It takes into account that socioeconomic attributes are often missing or unobserved and therefore they have to be treated as stochastic variables; and (2) it also assumes that the decision-maker (household) chooses an alternative under the condition of bounded rationality (Wal van Lierop, 1985). This suggests that each household maximizes utility rationally within the framework of personal criterial and a well-defined structure of preferences which are reflected in his personal utility function. It assumes that some attributes, which may be theoretically very important, may not be included in the personal utility function, as they are not preferred by the specific household. These elements of individual observations can lead to an unexplained part in the observed behaviour. Thus, different choices may be made by people who are facing exactly the same set of alternatives, described by exactly the same set of attributes; therefore the choice has to be considered partly as a random decision. Theoretically these problems can be tackled by assuming that individual utility, on which the choice of a specific alternative *i* is based, is a random variable, based on a set of arguments or a vector of explanatory variables. Let X_{in} denote the vector of explanatory variables. The utility function, $U(X_{in})$, can be represented as:

$$U(X_{in}) = V(X'_{in}\,\beta) + \eta\,(X'_{in}\,\gamma) + \xi_{in}$$

where

$\beta, \gamma =$ vectors of coefficients;

$V(X'_{in}\ \beta)$= deterministic function of the J' elements of the attribute vector X_{in} in which $J' \leq J$, representing the maximum number of attributes present. $V(X'_{in}\ \beta)$ defines the average utility of i for individual n. We assume $V(X'_{in}\ \beta)$ to be a linear combination of perceived values of the set of observed attributes.;

$\eta(X'_{in}\ \gamma)$= is a function of unexplained elements which are:

(a) Taste variations over the observed attributes;
(b) Individual measurement errors;
(c) Inconsistencies in the individual's choice behaviour, based on $V(X'_{in}\ \beta)$;
(d) Influences of the assumption of linearity of the strict utility function; and

ξ_{in} = a function of the influence on of missing, omitted, or unobserved attributes.

Since the last two terms $\eta(X'_{in}\ \gamma)$ and ξ_{in} are impossible to separate, they are always taken together in one disturbance term e_{in}. Therefore:

$$U(X_{in}) = V(X'_{in}\ \beta) + e_{in}\ ;\ i=1\ .\ .I,\ n=1\ .\ .N \tag{1}$$

The utility maximizing process can be described in the random utility approach as the evaluation process of the individual n of the utilities of all the available alternatives, i, U_{in}. We can make the following general probability statement for any chosen alternative i compared to all other alternatives.

$$P_{in} = Pr\ (U_{in} = Max\ (U_{i'n}))$$
$$P_{in} = Pr\ (U_{in} \geq U_{i'n},\ \forall_{i'});\ i,\ i' = 1\ .\ .\ .\ I;\ i \neq i';\ n=1\ .\ .\ .\ N \tag{2}$$

The above equation states that the probability that a random alternative i will be chosen by individual n is equal to the probability that the utility of i exceeds or equals the utility of any other alternative i for n. Thus, the household maximises utility.

If we substitute Equation (1) into Equation (2) we derive the final equation of the random utility approach, with a random specification.

$$P_{in} = Pr\,[V(X'_{in}\,\beta) + e_{in} \geq V(X'_{i'n}\,\beta) + e_{i'n}]$$
$$Pr[e_{i'n} \leq V(X'_{in}\,\beta) + e_{in} - V(X'_{i'n}\,\beta)] \qquad (3)$$

With the condition that:

$$\sum_{i=1}^{I} P_{in} = 1$$

The calculation of the choice probabilities depends heavily on the functional form chosen for Equation (3). In this respect, the distribution of the error term e_{in} plays an important role. In this study we assume that the distribution of the error term is independent and identically distributed (IID). The multinomial logic model (MNL) results from Equation (3), when it is assumed that the error terms are modeled by a set of variables which are:

(1) Mutually independent identically extreme value distributed.[1]
(2) Have zero mean and are uncorrelated with the perceived or directly measured attribute values and related parameters of the alternatives.
(3) Consistent with respect to maximisation

All of the above requirements are met by the "Gumbel" distribution which is a skewed distribution that can be almost normalised by using logarithms. This distribution has the following form:

$$Pr(\varepsilon_{i'n} \leq \varepsilon^*) = e^{-e^{-\varepsilon^*+\gamma}} \qquad (4)$$

where

$$\varepsilon = V(X'_{i'n}\,\beta) + \varepsilon_{in} - V(X'_{in}\,\beta)$$

and Υ is known as Euler's constant, $\Upsilon \approx 0.577$.

Assuming that Equation (4) is correct we can derive the multinominal logit model from Equation (3). (For the exact mathematical derivation, see McFadden, 1973).

$$P_{in} = \frac{e^V(X'_{in}\beta)}{\sum_{i=1}^{I} e^V(X'_{i'n}\beta)} \qquad (5)$$

The Choice Set

Housing is a heterogeneous commodity. Houses are built in many shapes and sizes, from single family houses to high-rise apartment buildings. A dwelling may have only a few rooms or many rooms. Houses can be rented or owned.

Sometimes it may suffice to express housing demand in terms of some aggregate unit of housing service, like housing expenditure divided by some form of quality corrected unit price. However, for policy purposes, the heterogeneity of housing cannot be ignored. The obvious heterogeneity of housing requires the application of discrete choice models in a description of housing demand that includes more than mere account of expenditure patterns. "Few people would argue that a family does not consider the quality of its potential neighbourhood or the menu of public services provided to that neighbourhood in its decision concerning what housing unit it will reside in" (Robertson C. Williams, 1979). Yet a number of studies have ignored this aspect in housing decisions (de Leenw and Ekanem, 1971). This omission has resulted from the assumption that housing is perfectly homogeneous, and hence no account need be taken of the different attributes which go into the housing choice decisions. The approach followed by these studies may be due to the fact that only aggregate housing data was available. However, it goes without saying that they ignore the fact that people do in fact care about the different attributes of the house they choose to live in.

In the model that is to be estimated we assume that the stock of housing varies with regard to quality and the characteristic of individual housing types. In a study of housing choice one of the most important dimensions of the study is to provide a set of choices faced by each household, or, establish a preference ordering of houses by households. The choice set, that is, the set of housing alternatives from which the household has to select one and only one, may become very large when many dimensions of housing are considered. Therefore, this study treats only the most important dimensions of housing as different categories that should be explained or predicted by the model. In order to overcome the problem of too many choices being set up which most statistical packages cannot handle well, two major dimensions of housing in the classification of dwellings into different types are considered:

(1) Structure Type (house or apartment); and
(2) Size of the Unit (measured by number of rooms).

Structure type is important in determining housing types and it is obvious that there is a vast difference between houses and apartments, the latter which are generally in high rise buildings in Rio. The size of the dwelling unit is taken into account next. The best measure of size is the floor space and lot size, however, this information was not available in the data set. Some studies have considered the number of bedrooms as a measure of size (Axel Borsch-Supan, 1987). In this study the total number of rooms has been used as a proxy measure for the size of the dwelling unit. This measure is superior to the total number of bedrooms, since it is much closer to the floor space variable. With these two characteristics being the most prominent in distinguishing dwelling units and with the objective of keeping the choice set to a manageable size, other characteristics have not been taken into account. Based on the structure type and size, dwelling units are classified into four different types:

House with One to Four Rooms = Smaller House
House with Five or More Rooms = Larger House
Apartment with One to Four Rooms = Smaller Apartment; and
Apartment with Five or More Rooms = Larger Apartment

The average number of rooms has been taken into account as the cut-off point for classifying the dwellings into four types. This classification was also chosen as it is more convenient in estimation.

Before proceeding to explain the equation to be estimated, some measurement issues common to all empirical studies need attention.

Explanatory Variables

In a typical housing demand equation, we distinguish three kinds of explanatory variables that describe the households satisfaction from consumption subject to a budget constraint: price and income variables that enter the budget constraint, a set of demographic factors that characterize measurable differences in preference among consumers, and the characteristics of the dwelling itself.

One of the major problems in estimating housing demand is the validity of the price variable entering into the budget constraint. Our data provide only monthly rents or monthly mortgage payments made by households; which are not the prices of the units. In a typical demand model, to use price variable we should have the purchase price or the market value of the house. The question then is whether rents or monthly mortgage payments can be used as a proxy for price. In a number of urban housing models the cost of a particular housing unit is treated as the price of the unit expressed as a monthly rental price. Because housing units are locationally fixed the price of the housing unit will vary across the metropolitan area. One could make an argument that because housing is a heterogeneous commodity, observed rents or monthly payments are not 'unit' prices but rather expenditures, i.e., the product of the price with the quantity of housing services consumed. The quantity of housing services consumed factors in the size of the dwelling, structural quality, and the level of amenities. In short, all features that contribute to the satisfaction form a dwelling. In this study, the approach we have taken is a deviation from some earlier studies which use hedonic rents and unit prices. In this study it is assumed that rents or monthly payments are attributes of the house types and that they are alternative specific. Thus, rents or monthly payments enter the utility function as attributes of the dwelling. That is, if the housing units are identical in all respects including location a household will pick the one with the lower rent. Thus, it is reflected as a characteristic of the house, rather than the price of the house.

The monthly payment variable is calculated as average monthly payment made by households which includes rents and cost of utilities. We have taken the average monthly figure since it is more representative of actual housing costs incurred. It also has the advantage of removing all fluctuations which occur due to varying utility bills over the year.

Household Income

When households choose a housing type to live in there are some monetary and psychic costs involved in the decision. Housing choice is likely to be dependent on a long term assessment of the financial and demographic circumstances. This suggests that the income variable should not only include current incomes but also expected incomes. This is likely to have a considerable effect on the specification of income (Quigley, 1979).

In any study the researcher is constrained by the available data, and this study is by no means an exception to that rule. The data set does not provide information on expected income for households.

Income measures relevant for long term housing decisions should not be influenced by transitory income fluctuations. Thus, in this study we have taken into account the average monthly income from all sources which includes wages and salaries, rents, pensions, dividends, and income from assets and investments. The income variable that enters the utility function as an explanatory variable is average monthly household income from all sources. Thus, it has been purged of monthly transitory income components by averaging. This averaging process makes the income variable close to the original permanent income concept (Friedman, 1987), although Friedman's permanent income concept averaged earnings and assets over the entire life time.

Demographic Variables

Demographic variables have been shown to be important in housing choice decisions. By including these variables the model can capture some taste variations among households. The variables included in this study are: age of the head of the household, size of the household, race of the head of the household, sex of the head of the household, as well as education and occupation of the household head. Most of the demographic variables enter the estimation in the form of dummies.

The household life cycle is an important predictor of housing choice. Housing consumption tends to rise with age but declines after retirement. Thus, the life cycle variable, age, is entered into the housing choice equation in a non-linear fashion, specifically as a parabola. We can capture this effect by include age and age squared as determinants of housing choice. The rent of the variables except for family size, enter the function only as dummy variables. All these household attributes are important in determining differences in utility functions between individual households. These factors are also likely to affect the utility associated with a particular dwelling unit. In addition, households might have preferences for housing characteristics that do not depend on any observed household attributes. However, the study assumes that, if important household attributes are included which we expect to affect preferences, the bulk of inter-household variation would be explained. A residual would undoubtedly remain, but it is likely to be relatively unimportant in comparison to the variations associated with observed characteristics. The importance of demographic variables and their specification issues are obvious. The reader is referred to McCarthy (1975) and the demographic literature for more details.

Locational Variables

Location of a dwelling is likely to influence the decision of households faced with a choice situation. In order to capture the spatial aspects in the process of decision-making, three dummy variables that are likely to capture the effect have been included. The study area has been divided into three sub-regions as has been explained in Chapter 4. Every effort was made to make these regions as distinct as possible. Dummy variables for these sub-regions will be included in the equation. Although, the literature suggests many other variables which could be included as a proxy for location, the data constraint does not permit such a possibility.

Database

This study concentrates on the housing choice in Rio municipality, which is in the state of Rio de Janeiro located in the South-west region of Brazil. The data employed are derived from the 1980 population census conducted by the Brazilian Institute for Geography and Statistics (IBGE). The IBGE was founded in 1938 to serve as the government's principal agency for the collection and analysis of data. Its responsibilities include conducting decennial demographic and economic censuses, annual household surveys, and collection of cost of living indices.

The IBGE stratifies urban Rio into eleven administrative regions, some of which comprise an aggregation of districts. The data has been taken from the one per cent sample of the population census for 1980, for the metropolitan region of Rio de Janeiro. There were approximately 2.5 million households residing in this area according to the 1980 census. There are approximately 25,000 units in the sample. This one per cent sample is a sub-sample of the 25 per cent sample, to which a larger questionnaire was applied. As all households were interviewed, the sample can be expanded to the universe with a high degree of accuracy. A statistical description of the data base is presented in Chapter 4.

Given these set of variables as defined in Table 5.1 the utility from a particular housing type '*i*' received by an individual'*n*' is given by the following expression.

$$\begin{aligned} U_{in} = &\beta_0 + \beta_1 \text{ MONTHPAY} + \beta_2 \text{ INCDOMI} + \beta_3 \text{ AGE} \\ &+ \beta_4 \text{ AGESQ} + \beta_5 \text{ DCOLOR} + \beta_6 \text{ DSCHOOL} \\ &+ \beta_7 \text{ DSCHOOL1} + \beta_8 \text{ DSCHOOL2} + \beta_9 \text{ NUBROOM} \\ &+ \beta_{10} \text{ DQUALITY} + \beta_{11} \text{ DAREA} + \beta_{12} \text{ DAREA1} \\ &+ \beta_{13} \text{ SIZFAMIL} + \beta_{14} \text{ DOCC} + \beta_{15} \text{ DOCC1} \\ &+ \beta_{16} \text{ DSEX} + e_{in}. \end{aligned}$$

TABLE 5.1: Definition of Variables

Variable	Definition
1. MONTHPAY	Rent or Monthly Mortagage Payments
2. INCDOMI	Average monthly household income
3. AGE	Age of the Head of the Household
4. AGESQ	Age Squire (Life Cycle Variable)
5. DCOLOR	1 if Household Head is White 0 otherwise
6. DSCHOOL	1 if Household Head has 12 or More Years of Schooling 0 otherwise
7. DSCHOOL1	1 if Household Head has 9 to 11 Years of Schooling 0 otherwise
8. DSCHOOL2	1 if Household Head has 4 to 8 Years of Schooling 0 otherwise
9. NUBROOM	Number of Bedrooms in the dwelling unit
10. DQUALITY	1 if the structure of the dwelling is of good quality 0 otherwise
11. DAREA	1 if Low Income Region 0 otherwise
12. DAREA1	1 if Middle Income Region 0 otherwise
13. SIZFAMIL	Size of the family
14. DOCC	1 if employment in professional and/or administrative occupatios 0 otherwise
15. DOCC1	1 if employed in Service or Transport 0 otherwise
16. DSEX	1 if male 0 otherwise

NOTE

1. Mensher and Johnson (1981) indicate that "independence indicates that the correlation between the unobserved attributes associated with each and every pair of alternatives in a choice set and across choice sets is zero. Identically distributed means that taste variations exist over the observed attributes. Yet it is neutral between alternatives, having the same distribution around the mean utility level.

6

STATISTICAL ESTIMATION AND EMPIRICAL RESULTS

Empirical Results of Multinomial Logit Model

The Multinomial Logit Model is estimated using the techniques of maximum likelihood estimation which has been explained in detail in the appendix. In this section only the results are presented and discussed. The model was estimated for three separate groups (all households, renters, and owners) classified by their income.

Based on studies in developed countries (Nijkamp, 1987; and Anas, 1981) several hypotheses have been offered concerning the sign and value of the parameter estimates which are presented in the tables. A positive sign of a variable would imply an increase in the probability of picking up a certain house type in relation to the omitted choice, given that all other factors influencing the decision are held unchanged. Monthly payment and income are expected to have a positive sign. Age and level of schooling are also expected to have a positive sign with the value of coefficients for a higher level of education to be higher than the value of coefficients for a lower level of education. The life cycle variables AGESQ is expected to have a negative sign, since we would expect households to prefer smaller units of housing in the later years of the life cycle to reduce maintenance and upkeeping costs. The two locational variables (DAREA and DAREA1) in the model are expected to have negative signs since they are less preferred areas. The race and sex variable of the head of the household are likely to have a positive sign, since it could be expected that males and whites would prefer larger sized houses or apartments. The variables number of rooms and quality of housing are expected to have a positive sign. Households may prefer larger housing and good quality housing over smaller and lower quality housing given everything else be unchanged. The variables measuring the size of the family and occupation are expected to have a positive sign.

Table 6.1 presents the results of the logit estimates for all households, Table 6.2 for all households with income less than 30,000 Cr. and Table 6.3 for all households with income greater than 30,000 Cr. The column labelled equation 1 presents the results for a relatively large house, Equation 2 for a relatively small apartment and lastly, Equation 3 for relatively large apartments. The estimated coefficients are presented for each equation with the value of the '*t*' statistic given in parentheses.

The coefficient for monthly payment and income are positive for the three equations for all income groups, with the exception of monthly payment variable for low income households in the first equation. This suggests that as rents or monthly payments rise, households tend to prefer larger units compared to smaller units. The coefficient for monthly payment is significant for smaller apartments and larger apartments for all income groups. for large houses, the coefficient is insignificant ($t <= 1.23$). The coefficient of the variable measuring the impact of household income is positive across all income groups and is significant in all cases except for smaller apartments for low income households. Table 6.1 suggests that as income rises, households on average will prefer larger houses and apartments over smaller houses with preference given to larger apartments.

The coefficient of the age variable is positive and significant for all households. The results suggest that households tend to prefer apartments or large houses as they move into the older age groups. However, the same trend is not true when the households are broken down by income group. Households with income less than 30,000 Cr. tend to prefer relatively larger houses and relatively smaller apartments. Although the coefficient for larger apartments is positive, it is insignificant. Those households with income greater than 30,000 Cr. still prefer apartments and relatively larger houses. These results confirm the fact that in Rio generally the households with low incomes live in houses and high income households live in apartments. This is contrary to the results of the studies done in developed countries like the United States and West Germany where the rich prefer houses and the poor prefer apartments. The life cycle variable, AGESQ has a negative sign for all three equations and for all income groups. This suggests that households tend to prefer smaller units of housing once they have reached their retirement age. In the beginning stages of life, households as they age tend to prefer larger units, both houses and apartments but, at late years they tend to cut back on their housing needs. A comparison of the coefficients of the AGE and AGESQ variable confirms this. These results tend to confirm the studies done in developed countries. However, a look at the '*t*' value suggests that all though we have across the board negative coefficients, they are significant only for small apartments, for all households, and households with less than 30,000 Cr. The coefficients are insignificant for households with greater than 30,000 Cr.

Three dummy variables have been included representing the level of education of the head of the household. The variable DSCHOOL represents households with twelve or more years of schooling, DSCHOOL1 represents households with eight to eleven years of schooling, and DSCHOOL2 represents households with four to seven years of schooling. An analysis of the results from Table 6.1 suggests that as the educational level of the head of household increases, households in general will have a stronger preference for larger units. It is also clear that households with higher levels of income prefer larger apartments over larger houses. In fact, apartments are preferred over houses for all levels of education. The coefficients for apartments are positive and greater than for houses. This fact reinforces the earlier suggestion that high income families tend to prefer apartments over houses. The coefficients are significant for all levels of education for larger apartments. However, their values fall with a decline in the educational level of the head of the household. The variables representing level of education in Table 6.2 which is for households with incomes less than 30,000 Cr. also suggest that households with higher levels of education tend to prefer larger units over smaller units; with higher preference for apartments over houses. The coefficients are significant only for the third equation (representing larger apartments) Table 6.3, representing households with greater than 30,000 Cr. of income suggests more or less a similar trend, with generally apartments having larger coefficient values compared to houses. However, the coefficients are significant for two higher levels of education only for apartments both larger and smaller.

The dummy variables are positive across all income groups capturing the effect of race of the head of the household, they are significant for all households and for households with income less than 30,000 Cr, but insignificant for households with incomes greater than 30,000 Cr. except for the third equation. The overall analysis suggests that whites are more likely to choose larger units compared to other races regardless of income groups. This trend is also seen across income groups.

The model also included variables that describe the characteristics of the houses. The major attributes included the following: the number of bedrooms (NUBROOM) and the quality of housing (DQUALITY) measured by the quality of material used in he construction of the unit. These variables were included in the model in the form of dummies. The coefficients for the variable, NUBROOM for all income groups are positive and very high for larger houses and larger apartments, but the same is not true in the case of smaller apartments. It is the latter which has a negative sign, except for high income groups. We find that as the number of bedrooms increases, households choose a larger unit with the value of the coefficient being larger for larger houses compared to larger apartments across income groups. The coefficient for households with less than 30,000 Cr., this variable has a negative sign for smaller apartments, which suggests that as the number of bedrooms increase, households with smaller apartments will prefer to move into smaller houses. There seems to be a justification for this result. It is possible that smaller houses have more bedrooms of smaller size, but this choice is not available in apartments. Apartments are constructed with a certain pattern and that cannot change from one unit to another unit. However, the same is not true to a house. It is not uncommon for two houses with the same amount of floor space to have different number of bedrooms. Thus, we would expect a movement from small apartments to small houses.

Housing quality is measured by the variable DQUALITY. As indicated by the significance of the coefficients, it appears that households place importance on the quality of housing. We also find from the tables that households who prefer better quality housing tend to choose apartments over houses. This would seem to be consistent with the reality since apartment complexes are constructed with more durable materials in the construction process. All the coefficients for this variable in the tables are significant. This suggests that households across all incomes prefer stronger and more durable housing units.

The dummy variable capturing the effect of the type of occupation are DOCC and DOCC1. DOCC represents households employed in Administrative and Professional occupations and DOCC1 represents households employed in Transport and Communication-related occupations. We find that (Table 6.1) households employed in

Professional and Administrative occupations are more likely to choose a larger unit with the coefficient for large apartments being larger than that for larger houses, indicating a greater preference for apartments. As has been indicated, apartments are located in the coastal parts of the city where most professional and administrative jobs are located. This tendency seems to be warranted. The coefficients are significant for both the larger apartments and larger houses. Although the coefficient for small apartments is also positive it is not significant.

The variable measuring the size of family is very erratic. Studies conducted in developed countries suggest that as the size of the family increases, households will tend to consume more housing space or prefer to choose larger units. However, as is indicated from Tables 6.1, 6.2 and 6.3 this does not seem to be the case in Rio. for all households (Table 6.1) none of the coefficients have a positive sign, suggesting that as the size of the family increases households will tend to move into smaller houses. In order to try to explain this result the sign of the coefficient was looked into (Table 6.2 and 6.3) or the SIZFAMIL variable for different income groups of households. This exercise also gives a negative sign across all the three equations. We also find that the coefficients are highly significant for all the three equations in each table. There are two possible explanations to this trend. First the data was collected over a period of one year and during this period (1979-1980) Brazil was under high inflationary pressure, in fact inflation increased 100 per cent almost every two to three months. Since this effect is not captured by our study we may see this type of erratic behaviour for this coefficient. Although we are holding monthly payments and incomes constant, they are really held constant only in nominal terms, but vary in real terms. In a country like Brazil incomes do not get adjusted contemporaneously inflation. However, we would expect landlords to raise rents as inflationary pressure builds. This results in a fall of real incomes of households. As the size of the family increases with real incomes falling, families would have to devote more of their income to meet other consumption needs and thus would choose to move into smaller units. A study conducted by Koth, Silva, and Dietz on housing in Latin America suggest that during this period of time the real rents in Rio were rising and real incomes were falling, although, in nominal terms incomes were held constant. This provides some clue to the sign of the coefficient.

The second explanation may be that in Rio, as in most developing countries, houses are built in bits and pieces and are not completed in one stretch. So even though households may be moving into smaller units they may be moving into units with a larger lot size with a possibility of future expansion which is not feasible in apartment units. A close look at the data was also taken in order to find clues to explain the behaviour for this variable. Data clearly show that households with low incomes tend to live in houses and also have large families. On the other hand, households with higher incomes and small families live in apartments. A large part of our data (about 50%) is for low income large family households. This may have an effect on the negative value of the coefficient for family size. The above observations are only a hypothetical. In any research, a stage may come where the researcher becomes a victim of the data set. In order to make any positive statement about this variable more information is needed on the structure of the housing markets in Rio which is not available at this time in the data set. In order to be able to explain this reality, a much more rigorous analysis is required on the structure of the housing market in Rio. This is beyond the scope of and is this study, therefore, left as an opening for future work in this area. Table 6.1 indicates that for all households, male heads are more likely to prefer larger units. There is also an indication that high income male household heads prefer apartments over houses.

The last set of variables needing explanation are the two locational variables: DAREA (Low Income Region) and DAREA1 (Middle Income Region). There is clear evidence that households tend to prefer good locations over inferior locations. The high income households tend to prefer houses over apartments if they live in low and middle income regions (Table 6.2). The coefficients for apartments are negative with '*t*' values being significant only for smaller apartments, except for larger apartments with higher income households. There is also an indication that high income households who choose to live in large houses prefer low and moderate income regions over high income regions.

Goodness of Fit Measures

In this section we will discuss the overall performance of the model. Author has used to measures: (1) Likelihood Ratio Index and (2) Percentage Correctly Predicted (PCP) to measure the predictability of the model. The Likelihood Ratio Index is often used in quantitative choice models to measure how well the model fits the data. The statistic measures how well the model, with its estimated parameters, performs compared with the model in which all the parameters are zero. This comparison is made on the basis of the Log Likelihood function evaluated at both the estimated parameters and at zero for all parameters.

This Likelihood Ratio Index is defined as:

$$\rho^2 = 1 - [LL(\beta^*) / LL(0)]$$

where $LL(\beta^*)$ is the value of the log likelihood function at the estimated parameters and $LL(0)$ is its value when all the parameters are set equal to zero. If the estimated parameters do no better, in terms of the likelihood function, than zero parameters then, $LL(\beta^*) = LL(0)$ and thus, $\rho^2 = 0$. This is the lowest value that ρ^2 can take.

The second goodness of fit measure that author has used is the Per cent Correctly Predicted: The per cent of the sampled decision-maker for which the model correctly predicts the actual decision made. This statistic is calculated by identifying for each sample the alternative with the highest probability based on the estimated model, and determining whether or not this was the alternative actually chosen.

For all models, the Likelihood Ratio Index and the PCP are presented in the tables. for all households the Likelihood Ratio Index is 0.43, for households with income greater than 30,000 Cr. It is 0.37, and 0.36 for households with income less than 30,000 Cr. Based on other studies done in the area of housing choice, the Likelihood Ratio Index above 0.30 is considered to be a reasonably good fit. for all households the model predicted 69.8 per cent correctly compared to 81 per cent for high income households and 67 per cent for low income households. Comparing the three tables we also notice that the prediction are not equally good for the four types of units. Table 6.1 indicates that the model prediction are better for smaller houses and larger apartments (77.4% and 80.8%, respectively). Only 60.3 per cent are predicted correctly for larger houses and 41.4 per cent for smaller apartments. for all households with income greater than 30,000 Cr., over all the models predictions are better for larger units, where the vast majority of households live, compared to smaller units. The model predicts 80.2 per cent correctly for smaller houses for low income households (Table 6.3), but only 46.2 per cent for smaller apartments.

TABLE 6.1: **Multinomial Logit Results for All Households**

Variable	Coeff (EQ 1) Larger House	Coeff (EQ 2) Smaller Apt.	Coeff (EQ 3) Larger Apt.
ASC	–6.60	–2.31	–7.415
	–(13.88)***	–(3.90)***	–(13.13)***
MONTHPAY	0.0000262	0.000136	0.000136
	(1.23)	(5.98)***	(6.32)***
INCDOMI	0.0000397	0.000262	0.0000405
	(10.01)***	(5.94)***	(10.11)***
AGE	0.0549	0.104	0.0613
	(2.95)**	(4.13)***	(2.75)**
AGESQ	–0.000262	–0.0011	–0.000321
	–(1.40)	–(4.20)***	–(1.44)
DCOLOR	0.586	0.451	0.932
	(6.31)***	(3.42)***	(7.61)***
DSCHOOL	0.539	0.667	1.520
	(2.08)**	(2.31)**	(5.73)***
DSCHOOL1	0.187	0.267	1.022
	(1.14)	(1.34)	(5.77)***
DSCHOOL2	0.0996	0.226	0.792
	(0.85)	(1.46)	(5.79)***
NUBROOM	2.277	–0.357	1.953
	(23.79)***	–(2.42)**	(18.36)***
DQUALITY	0.914	2.422	3.247
	(0.07)***	(16.84)***	(23.82)***
DAREA	0.238	–2.472	–1.173
	(1.52)	–(12.74)***	–(6.83)***
DAREA1	–0.271	–1.697	–1.093
	–(1.78)	–(11.28)***	–(7.18)***
DSEX	0.305	–0.073	0.0644
	(2.60)***	–(0.49)	(0.47)
SIZFAMIL	–0.222	–0.305	–0.275
	–(7.14)***	–(5.83)***	–(6.68)***
DOCC	0.310	0.346	0.513
	(2.14)**	(1.98)*	(3.28)***
DOCC1	0.0249	–0.233	0.0316
	(0.23)	–(1.51)	–(0.229)

LOG-LIKELIHOOD.. –4552.1
RESTRICTED (SLOPE =0) LOG-L.. –8095.9
CHI-SQUARE.. 7087.6
DEGREES OF FREEDOM... 48

$$\rho^2 = 1 - \frac{L^*(\beta)}{L^*(0)} = 1 - .57 = 0.43$$

(Contd.)

PCP = 69.8

ACTUAL	TOTAL	PREDICTED 0	1	2	3	%
TOTAL	6167	1861	1636	470	2200	
0	1708	1323	279	62	44	77.4
1	1817	347	1096	35	339	60.3
2	623	157	23	258	185	41.4
3	2019	34	238	115	1632	80.8

Note: * Coefficient significant at .10.
** Coefficient significant at .05.
*** Coefficient significant at .01.

TABLE 6.2: Multinomial Logit Results for Households with Income Greater than 30,000 Cr.

Variable	Coeff (EQ 1) Larger House	Coeff (EQ 2) Smaller Apt.	Coeff (EQ 3) Larger Apt.
ASC	–7.85	–3.570	–7.43
	–(4.67)***	–(1.91)*	–(4.41)***
MONTHPAY	0.0000359	0.000103	0.000114
	(0.86)	(2.43)**	(2.78)**
INCDOMI	0.0000250	0.0000117	0.0000240
	(2.90)**	(1.31)	(2.79)**
AGE	0.0671	0.0809	0.0788
	(1.07)	(1.15)	(1.25)
AGESQ	–0.000328	–0.000673	–0.000520
	–(0.52)	–(0.95)	–(0.83)
DCOLOR	0.467	0.392	0.740
	(1.59)	(1.07)	(2.43)**
DSCHOOL	0.5977	1.180	1.301
	(1.32)	(2.30)**	(2.87)**
DSCHOOL1	0.5521	1.015	1.226
	(1.35)	(2.13)**	(2.97)**
DSCHOOL2	0.2113	0.630	0.662
	(0.63)	(1.51)	(1.93)*
NUBROOM	2.721	0.0360	2.232
	(9.85)***	(0.11)	(8.04)***
DQUALITY	0.974	2.534	3.227
	(2.88)**	(6.45)***	(9.56)***
DAREA	- 1.134	–2.334	–0.330
	(2.52)**	–(3.65)***	–(0.73)

(Contd)

TABLE 6.2 *(Contd.)*

Variable	Coeff (EQ 1) Larger House	Coeff (EQ 2) Smaller Apt.	Coeff (EQ 3) Larger Apt.
DAREA1	0.550	–1.043	–0.413
	(1.34)	–(2.45)**	–(0.63)
DSEX	0.524	0.0788	0.233
	(1.46)	(0.19)	(3.96)***
SIZFAMIL	–0.232	–0.260	–0.359
	–(3.69)***	–(2.20)***	–(3.96)***
DOCC	0.200	0.800	0.492
	(0.61)	(2.09)**	(1.49)
DOCC1	0.119	0.826	0.199
	(0.35)	(1.86)*	(0.52)

LOG-LIKELIHOOD.. –1523.2
RESTRICTED (SLOPE = 0) LOG-L...–2388.2
CHI-SQUARE.. 1730.1
DEGREES OF FREEDOM.. 48

$$\rho^2 = 1 - \frac{L^*(\beta)}{L^*(0)} = 1 - .64 = 0.36$$

PCP = 81.0

		PREDICTED				
ACTUAL	TOTAL	0	1	2	3	%
TOTAL	2240	66	607	74	1673	
0	95	32	43	4	16	33.6
1	688	17	433	4	234	62.9
2	184	10	8	47	119	25.5
3	1435	7	133	19	1304	89.7

TABLE 6.3: Multinomial Logit Results for All Households with Income Less than 30,000 Cr.

Variable	Coeff (EQ 1) Larger House	Coeff (EQ 2) Smaller Apt.	Coeff (EQ 3) Larger Apt.
ASC	–6.403	–1.97	–7.58
	–(12.53)	–(2.93)	(10.40)
MONTHPAY	–0.0000101	0.000186	0.000149
	–(0.878)	(6.14)***	(5.10)***

(Contd)

TABLE 6.3 *(Contd.)*

Variable	Coeff (EQ 1) Larger House	Coeff (EQ 2) Smaller Apt.	Coeff (EQ 3) Larger Apt.
INCDOMI	0.0000440	0.0000308	0.0000767
	(5.82)***	(2.82)**	(7.20)***
AGE	0.0576	0.108	0.0282
	(2.90)**	(3.73)***	(1.00)
AGESQ	–0.000289	–0.00120	0.0000648
	–(1.45)	–(3.93)***	(0.23)
DCOLOR	0.626	0.432	0.903
	(6.32)***	(2.95)**	(5.78)***
DSCHOOL	0.703	0.495	1.724
	(1.94)*	(1.26)	(4.53)***
DSCHOOL1	0.179	0.0301	0.839
	(0.955)	(0.13)	(3.68)***
DSCHOOL2	0.120	0.141	0.874
	(0.95)	(0.81)	(5.09)***
NUBROOM	2.16	–0.472	2.06
	(20.88)***	–(2.54)	(14.40)***
DQUALITY	1.02	2.436	3.385
	(7.07)***	(15.28)***	(19.98)***
DAREA	0.0698	–2.461	–1.325
	(0.41)	–(11.88)	–(6.23)***
DAREA1	–0.406	–1.80	–1.2050
	–(2.40)***	–(10.76)***	–(6.46)***
DSEX	0.247	–0.0997	–0.0283
	(1.96)*	(0.59)	–(0.116)
SIZFAMIL	–0.201	–0.352	–0.315
	–(5.92)***	–(5.68)***	–(5.32)***
DOCC	0.451	0.209	0.425
	(2.70)**	(0.99)	(2.07)**
DOCCI	0.0511	–0.442	0.159
	(0.44)	–(2.55)**	(0.89)

LOG-LIKELIHOOD.. –2962.7
RESTRICTED (SLOPE = 0) LOG-L.. –4725.0
CHI-SQUARE.. 3524.6
DEGREES OF FREEDOM.. 48

$$\rho^2 = 1 - \frac{L^*(\beta)}{L^*(0)} = 1 - .63 = 0.37$$

PCP = 67.0

(Contd.)

		PREDICTED				
ACTUAL	TOTAL	0	1	2	3	%
TOTAL	3747	1801	1032	372	541	
0	1613	1295	236	58	24	80.2
1	1129	329	671	30	99	59.4
2	439	145	14	203	77	46.2
3	566	32	111	82	341	60.2

Analysis of Renter Households

In this section an analysis of renter households is presented. Renter and owner households are analyzed separately to see if there exist major differences between the two groups which may not be captured by the analysis of all households. Tables 6.4, 6.5, and 6.6 pertain to all renters and renters with incomes less than and greater than 30,000 Cr. Looking at the coefficients for income and monthly payments we find that they all have a positive sign and are statistically significant. This suggests that as rents and incomes rise, households will choose larger houses or apartments. Larger apartments have large coefficient for income compared to larger houses except for high income households indicating that the household preference is more toward apartments in the same category rather than houses. The variable, AGESQ is negative for in the equations for all renters (Table 6.4); suggesting that as renter households move into the retirement age they choose to live in smaller houses. However, the same is not true for renters classified by income groups. There is a clear indication from Table 6.6 that high income households do not prefer smaller houses, they continue to show inclination toward larger units or apartments in general. All the coefficients are positive but are statistically insignificant. Thus, we cannot make any strong statements regarding this variable for this particular group of renters. The coefficient for the low income households (Table 6.5) is negative only for larger houses and smaller apartments. However, it is significant only in the case of smaller apartments suggesting that renters of smaller apartments will prefer choosing smaller houses as one ages. The coefficients for the race variable (DCOLOR) are positive in all three tables but they are not significant in general for the high income renters. Household heads who are white tend to choose larger units irrespective of the structure type.

Table 6.4 indicates that households who have twelve or more years of schooling (DSCHOOL) are more likely to choose a larger dwelling with greater preference towards large apartments compared to large houses. However, smaller houses are preferred to smaller apartments for the same group of renter households. Low income renters (<30,000 Cr.) with twelve or more years of schooling prefer large houses or larger apartments over smaller houses and smaller apartments. Both the coefficients are positive, but they are not significant. In fact, all the coefficients for all levels of education are insignificant for low income renters (Table 6.5). This gives an indication that level of education may not play a major role in housing choice decisions for low income renters. The coefficients, DSCHOOL (12+ years), DSCHOOL1 (9 to 11 years), and DSCHOOL2 (4 to 8 years) are all positive for high income renters (Table 6.6). This suggests that irrespective of the level of education high income renters prefer larger houses and any size of apartments over small houses. With this group of households, those with high levels of education show a greater preference towards later apartments over larger houses. The coefficients are significant only for larger apartments for the highest and lowest educational group. Thus, no strong statements can be made for any of the other types of housing.

The coefficients of the locational variables DAREA (middle income region) and DAREA1 (low income region) are all negative except for the larger house for both income groups in the middle income region. This suggests that as far as the location is concerned, all renters will choose a smaller unit in good locations rather than large units in inferior locations, with the exception of high income renters who prefer large houses in the middle income region. Households tend to trade off housing characteristics for locational advantage like proximity to work, public schools, and other public services. We also notice that all the coefficients for the locational variable in Table 6.4 are significant with the exception of the larger houses in the middle income region. The same trend exists for low income renter households. However, only the smaller apartment variable is significant for higher income renters.

The coefficient of the size of the family variable shows major differences when compared with the coefficient of all households. Overall, as the size of a family increases renters prefer houses to apartments. In addition, they also prefer smaller houses to larger houses. Similar trends exist for low income renters (Table 6.5). We find that as the size of the family increases apartment dwellers will prefer moving into housing units which may be smaller than apartment units, suggesting their preference for more open space. High income renters tend to behave in a different way (Table 6.6). The coefficients are negative, except for smaller apartments. This suggests that high income renters will prefer an apartment over a house. Table 6.6 also suggests that they will prefer a smaller apartment to a larger apartment since the coefficient for the larger apartment equation is larger. A look at the t-values suggests that none of the coefficients are significant. Thus, one has to refrain from making any strong statements.

The variable DOCC (Administrative and Professional Occupation) has a positive coefficient in all the tables. Thus, the value of the coefficient would suggest that renters employed in administrative and professional occupations would prefer larger houses and apartments in general over smaller houses. Their inclination is more toward apartments compared to even larger houses (coefficient for smaller apartment and larger apartments is greater than for larger houses. Table 6.4, however the coefficients are all insignificant. We also find that low income renters employed in professional occupations tend to prefer larger units over smaller houses but would also choose smaller apartments over smaller houses. Their preference is, however, inclined towards larger houses over apartments (the coefficient for DOCC is greater for larger houses compared to apartments). The t values do not indicate that the coefficients are significant, however, it remains our belief that in Rio low income households prefer houses over apartments which was suggested earlier. Table 6.6 indicates that high income renters are more likely to choose apartments over houses with a greater preference for smaller apartments irrespective of the type of occupation they are employed in.

The coefficient of the number of bedrooms (NUBROOM) variable is significant and high for larger houses and larger apartments but is negative for smaller apartments suggesting that households will tend to choose smaller houses over smaller apartments (Table 6.4). The coefficient for larger houses is higher than for larger apartments, reinforcing our belief that renters in general prefer houses over apartments. Renters who place importance on the quality of the structure of the unit are more likely to live in apartment units, the quality coefficients for the apartment units are high and very significant, but insignificant for larger houses. This is also true for both low income and high income renters. Another variable of interest is the sex of the head of the household. We find that male household heads prefer smaller houses to smaller apartments.

Overall, the model's prediction increases when the analysis is done separately for renter households. for all renters, the Log Likelihood Ratio is 0.44 and Per cent Correctly Predicted is 69.7. The Model's Predictions are very good for small houses and large apartments (81.8 and 79.2, respective). The Likelihood Ratio for low income renters is 0.37 and the model predicts 67.9 per cent correctly. The best prediction of the model is for the high income households where the Log Likelihood Ratio Index is 0.40 and the predictions are 74.7 per cent correct. Compared to the analysis of all households we find that overall the model predicts best for high income households, 80 per cent for all high income households, and 74.7 per cent for all high income renter households. We have gained some insight into the inconsistencies of the variable for the family size through this exercise and that is the major difference that we have found for the renters compared to all households.

TABLE 6.4: Multinomial Logit Results for all Renters

Variable	Coeff (EQ 1) Larger House	Coeff (EQ 2) Smaller Apt.	Coeff (EQ 3) Larger Apt.
ASC	–6.95	–0.999	–7.767
	–(9.4)	–(1.37)	–(9.06)
MONTHPAY	0.000210	0.000187	0.000318
	(6.73)***	(5.73)***	(9.99)***
INCDOMI	0.0000286	0.0000268	0.0000335
	(4.64)***	(4.16)***	(5.38)***
AGE	0.0546	0.0946	0.0487
	(1.88)*	(2.96)**	(1.46)
AGESQ	–0.000263	–0.00106	–0.000243
	–(0.88)	–(3.12)***	–(0.77)
DCOLOR	0.722	0.363	1.051
	(4.79)***	(2.24)**	(5.46)***
DSCHOOL	0.536	–0.144	0.860
	(1.47)	–(0.39)	(2.32)**
DSCHOOL1	0.155	–0.339	0.395
	(0.66)	–(1.35)	–(1.55)
DSCHOOL2	0.141	–0.152	0.157
	(0.77)	–(0.76)	(0.73)
NUBROOM	2.114	–0.645	1.744
	(13.54)**	–(3.19)***	(10.14)***

(Contd)

TABLE 6.4 *(Contd.)*

Variable	Coeff (EQ 1) Larger House	Coeff (EQ 2) Smaller Apt.	Coeff (EQ 3) Larger Apt.
DQUALITY	0.297	2.081	2.967
	(1.51)	(11.65)***	(14.39)***
DAREA	–0.401	–2.768	–0.981
	–(1.55)	–(11.11)***	–(3.41)***
DAREA1	–0.848	–2.011	–1.00
	–(3.45)***	–(9.96)***	–(4.21)***
DSEX	0.612	–0.111	0.116
	(3.07)***	–(0.58)	(0.55)
SIZFAMIL	–0.159	–0.285	–0.218
	–(2.96)**	–(4.26)***	–(3.26)***
DOCC	0.178	0.310	0.361
	(0.86)	(1.43)	(1.63)
DOCC1	–0.0380	–0.297	0.0731
	–(0.22)	–(1.56)	(0.34)

LOG-LIKELIHOOD.. –1936.8
RESTRICTED (SLOPE = 0) LOG-L.......................................–3456.8
CHI-SQUARE.. 3040.1
DEGREES OF FREEDOM.. 48

$$\rho^2 = 1 - \frac{L^*(\beta)}{L^*(0)} = 1 - .56 = 0.44$$

PCP = 69.7

		PREDICTED				
ACTUAL	TOTAL	0	1	2	3	%
TOTAL	2558	993	366	438	761	
0	880	720	74	63	23	81.8
1	498	149	224	25	100	44.9
2	462	111	11	271	69	58.6
3	718	13	57	79	569	79.2

TABLE 6.5: Multinomial Logit Results for Renters with Income Less than 30,000 Cr.

Variable	Coeff (EQ 1) Larger House	Coeff (EQ 2) Smaller Apt.	Coeff (EQ 3) Larger Apt.
ASC	–7.140	–1.188	–8.319
	–(8.71)	–(1.44)	–(7.17)
MONTHPAY	0.000213	0.000186	0.000296
	(5.71)***	(4.65)***	(7.11)***
INCDOMI	0.0000256	0.0000125	0.0000717
	(2.00)**	(0.88)	(4.14)***

(Contd)

TABLE 6.5 *(Contd.)*

Variable	Coeff (EQ 1) Larger House	Coeff (EQ 2) Smaller Apt.	Coeff (EQ 3) Larger Apt.
AGE	0.0628	0.125	0.0264
	(2.00)**	(0.88)	(4.14)***
AGESQ	–0.000307	–0.00147	0.0000312
	–(0.96)	–(3.715)***	(0.72)
DCOLOR	0.788	0.385	1.095
	(4.77)***	(2.18)**	(4.34)***
DSCHOOL	0.574	–0.280	0.618
	(1.08)	–(0.58)	(1.12)
DSCHOOL1	0.237	–0.485	–0.0295
	(0.89)	–(1.66)	–(0.08)
DSCHOOL2	0.0937	–0.162	0.0309
	(0.46)	–(0.73)	(1.120)
NUBROOM	1.974	0.529	1.941
	(11.14)***	(2.19)**	(8.70)***
DQUALITY	0.353	2.143	3.241
	(1.54)	(10.86)***	(11.96)***
DAREA	0.488	–2.749	–0.780
	–(1.73)*	–(10.61)***	–(2.18)**
DAREA1	–0.790	–2.101	–0.910
	–(2.88)**	–(9.64)***	–(3.66)***
DSEX	0.671	–0.0738	–0.0388
	(3.05)***	–(0.35)	(0.14)
SIZFAMIL	–0.121	–0.357	–0.319
	–(1.95)*	–(4.56)***	–(3.19)***
DOCC	0.306	0.297	0.256
	(1.27)	(1.19)	(0.87)
DOCCI	–0.0325	–0.500	0.154
	–(0.17)	–(2.38)**	(0.55)

LOG-LIKELIHOOD.. –1324.9
RESTRICTED (SLOPE = 0) LOG-L... –2106.5
CHI-SQUARE.. 1563.4
DEGREES OF FREEDOM.. 48

$$\rho^2 = 1 - \frac{L^*(\beta)}{L^*(0)} = 1 - .63 = 0.37$$

PCP = 67.9

Contd.

ACTUAL	TOTAL	PREDICTED 0	1	2	3	%
TOTAL	1689	953	199	309	228	
0	824	693	58	58	15	84.1
1	311	144	112	17	38	36.0
2	336	107	6	195	28	58.0
3	218	9	23	39	147	67.4

TABLE 6.6: Multinomial Logit Results for All Renters with Income Greater than 30,000 Cr.

Variable	Coeff (EQ 1) Larger House	Coeff (EQ 2) Smaller Apt.	Coeff (EQ 3) Larger Apt.
ASC	–7.007	–2.027	–7.326
	–(2.79)	–(0.77)	–(2.93)
MONTHPAY	0.000257	0.000266	0.000366
	(3.75)***	(3.74)***	(5.37)***
INCDOMI	0.0000328	0.0000292	0.0000312
	(2.07)**	(1.83)*	(1.98)**
AGE	–0.0246	–0.0195	0.00935
	–(0.25)	–(0.19)	(0.09)
AGESQ	0.000507	0.000381	0.000333
	(0.50)	(0.36)	(0.33)
DCOLOR	0.0383	0.154	0.753
	(0.89)	(0.31)	(1.68)*
DSCHOOL	1.032	0.934	1.358
	(1.62)	(1.35)	(2.13)**
DSCHOOL1	0.457	0.663	0.943
	(0.77)	(1.02)	(1.61)
DSCHOOL2	0.678	0.515	0.307
	(0.95)	(0.81)	(5.09)***
NUBROOM	2.494	–0.701	1.835
	(6.52)***	–(1.58)	(4.79)***
DQUALITY	0.373	2.328	2.914
	(0.78)	(4.38)***	(6.17)***
DAREA	0.549	–2.932	–0.379
	(0.64)	–(2.69)**	–(0.45)
DAREA1	–0.401	–1.437	–0.650
	–(0.52)	–(1.96)*	–(0.89)
DSEX	0.271	–0.501	–0.166
	(0.46)	–(0.84)	–(0.93)
SIZFAMIL	–0.106	0.0318	–0.0923
	–(0.85)	(0.20)	–(0.70)
DOCC	0.317	1.197	0.719
	(0.69)	(2.26)**	(1.55)
DOCCI	0.720	1.588	0.982
	(1.31)	(2.58)**	(1.78)*

(Contd.)

LOG-LIKELIHOOD.. –574.15
RESTRICTED (SLOPE = 0) LOG-L...–960.51
CHI-SQUARE... 772.72
DEGREES OF FREEDOM.. 48

$$\rho^2 = 1 - \frac{L^*(\beta)}{L^*(0)} = 1 - .60 = 0.40$$

PCP = 74.7

		PREDICTED				
ACTUAL	TOTAL	0	1	2	3	%
TOTAL	'869	42	170	122	535	
0	56	24	17	7	8	42.8
1	187	8	114	8	57	60.9
2	126	5	5	79	37	62.7
3	500	5	34	28	433	86.6

Analysis of Owner Households

This section of the analysis deals exclusively with owner occupied households. As has been mentioned earlier, this type of an analysis allows us to capture the differences in the decision-making process for renters and owners separately which may not be possible when all households are viewed as making identical decisions.

As with the case of renter households, we find from Tables 6.8, 6.9, and 6.10 that the monthly payment and the income coefficients are positive except for the income variable in equation 2 in Table 6.9. It should be pointed out that the monthly payment for owners were calculated as monthly payments including taxes. But there was no information available for down-payments, so that we could not make any adjustments in the data. Therefore, the monthly payment variable should be interpreted with caution. The analysis suggest that as monthly payments and incomes increase, households will choose to own larger units of the dwelling. We also find that for all households (Table 6.7) the (MONTHPAY) coefficient for large apartments and smaller apartments are both larger than for larger houses suggesting that households may prefer owning apartment units over houses. Table 6.9 indicates that for high income owners none of the coefficients of income or monthly payments are significant. for low income owners with the coefficient being higher for larger apartments than for larger houses. This suggests that low income owners, will prefer to own larger apartments over large houses but would prefer larger houses to smaller houses. The race variable DCOLOR is positive and highly significant for all owner-households and households with low incomes. These results are consistent with studies done in the Philippines and Korea. White households heads choose larger units of a dwelling compared to non-Whites. Whites also tend to place more emphasis on apartments over houses. This is due to the fact that we find Whites being the ones with high incomes located in high income regions where apartments are considered superior to houses. Most of the coefficients measuring the level of schooling of the head of the household are positive and significant for all households and for low income owners with a few exceptions. The tables suggest that as the level of schooling increases, owners are more likely to choose larger units — of apartments both in smaller and larger apartment categories compared to smaller houses. Households with twelve or more years of schooling are more likely to choose an apartment unit over a house. Low income owners (Table 6.8) prefer apartments in general and larger houses as the level of schooling rises, with their preference higher for apartments over houses. They also prefer larger units within the respective categories. Based on Table 6.9 none of the schooling coefficients are significant. Although, the value of the coefficients suggest that they would prefer both larger houses and apartments in general. They place greater importance on larger apartments and/or smaller apartments over larger houses.

Location seems to be a very significant determinant of housing choice for the owner group. Owner's who choose to live in inferior locations tend to choose houses over apartments. We find that the coefficients, DAREA and DAREA1 are negative for apartments (Table 6.7). This suggests a preference for smaller houses over apartments. We also find from Table 6.9 that high income owners prefer to choose larger houses if they live in moderate or low income regions. The coefficients are both high and significant. Occupation of the head of the household is important in housing choice decisions. Household heads who are employed in professional and administrative occupations (DOCC) are likely to choose larger units of dwellings with a greater preference for larger apartments reflected in the coefficient for larger apartments. The coefficients are significant in general for larger units, however, none are significant for high income owners.

Households place a great importance on the size of the dwelling measured by the number of bedrooms and the quality of the structure. Over all income groups we find that households who prefer good-quality structures tend to choose apartments over houses. However, they are more likely to choose larger houses compared to larger apartments as far as when an increase in the number of bedrooms is concerned. The coefficient for the size of the family is negative across all incomes for all the equations. A glance at Table 6.9 suggests that as the size of the family increases, high income owner households tend to choose houses over apartments. This is possible due to the fact that there are possibilities of future expansion of the units.

Overall the model performs well. The Likelihood Ratio for all owners is 0.44, 0.40 for low income owners and 0.35 for high income owners. Again, as in the case of renters and all households, the model then predicts best for the high income owners: 77.8 per cent compared to only 69.7 per cent for low income owners and 68 per cent for all the owner households. Table 6.7 also indicates that the model predicts best for the larger apartments (84.0%). for the larger apartments in the low income owners the model predicts 70.6 per cent for the low income owners and 90.2 per cent for high income owners.

TABLE 6.7: Multinomial Logit Results for Owner-Occupied Houses

Variable	Coeff (EQ 1) Larger House	Coeff (EQ 2) Smaller Apt.	Coeff (EQ 3) Larger Apt.
ASC	–6.417	–6.30	–6.810
	–(9.53)	–(5.21)	–(8.19)
MONTHPAY	0.000241	0.000348	0.000371
	(2.75)**	(3.88)***	(4.22)***
INCDOMI	0.0000386	0.0000261	0.0000384
	(6.93)***	(4.07)***	(6.83)***
AGE	0.0528	0.161	0.0491
	(2.02)**	(3.33)***	(1.51)
AGESQ	–0.000269	–0.00145	–0.000244
	–(1.04)	–(3.03)***	–(0.76)
DCOLOR	0.495	0.775	0.850
	(3.97)***	(2.95)**	(5.03)***
DSCHOOL	0.979	2.311	2.129
	(2.11)**	(4.31)***	(4.48)***
DSCHOOLI	0.670	1.416	1.739
	(2.41)**	(3.75)***	(5.88)***

(Contd)

TABLE 6.7 *(Contd.)*

Variable	Coeff (EQ 1) Larger House	Coeff (EQ 2) Smaller Apt.	Coeff (EQ 3) Larger Apt.
DSCHOOL2	0.0998	0.891	1.088
	(0.614)	(3.32)	(5.70)**
NUBROOM	2.279	–0.00494	1.940
	(18.10)***	–(0.02)	(13.8)***
DQUALITY	1.310	2.88	3.513
	(6.66)***	(10.61)***	(16.99)***
DAREA	0.642	–1.929	–1.096
	(3.07)***	–(5.55)***	–(4.74)***
DAREA1	0.199	–1.181	–0.823
	(0.956)	–(4.55)***	–(3.80)***
«PG»			
DSEX	0.186	–0.0785	0.0461
	(1.19)*	–(0.30)	(0.24)
SIZFAMIL	–0.256	–0.274	–0.299
	–(6.47)***	–(2.81)**	–(5.50)***
DOCC	0.529	0.403	0.772
	(2.33)**	(1.26)	(3.14)***
DOCC1	0.0611	0.0128	–0.00152
	(0.42)	(0.04)	–(0.008)

LOG-LIKELIHOOD.. –2432.2
RESTRICTED (SLOPE = 0) LOG-L .... –4374.7
CHI-SQUARE.. 3885.1
DEGREES OF FREEDOM.. 48

$$\rho^2 = 1 - \frac{L^*(\beta)}{L^*(0)} = 1 - .56 = 0.44$$

PCP = 74.7

		PREDICTED				
ACTUAL	TOTAL	0	1	2	3	%
TOTAL	3609	844	1286	18	1461	
0	828	615	186	2	25	74.2
1	1319	182	902	2	233	68.3
2	161	29	12	11	109	6.8
3	1301	18	186	3	1094	84.0

TABLE 6.8: **Multinomial Logit Results for All Owners with Income Less than 30.000 Cr.**

Variable	Coeff (EQ 1) Larger House	Coeff (EQ 2) Smaller Apt.	Coeff (EQ 3) Larger Apt.
ASC	–5.884	–6.027	–6.589
	–(8.30)	–(4.10)	–(6.14)
MONTHPAY	0.000166	0.000752	0.000860
	(1.29)	(5.46)***	(6.61)***
INCDOMI	0.0000501	0.0000546	0.0000833
	(5.02)***	(2.81)**	(5.59)***
AGE	0.0460	0.142	–0.0148
	(1.69)*	(2.43)**	–(0.35)
AGESQ	–0.000217	–0.00121	0.000457
	–(0.80)	–(2.10)	(1.25)
DCOLOR	0.518	0.675	0.803
	(3.97)***	(2.19)***	(3.58)***
DSCHOOL	1.399	2.766	2.716
	(2.06)**	(3.52)***	(3.79)***
DSCHOOL1	0.512	1.452	1.657
	(1.62)	(3.17)***	(4.48)***
DSCHOOL2	0.139	0.832	1.012
	(0.79)	(2.61)**	(4.52)***
NUBROOM	2.169	–0.486	1.997
	(16.32)***	–(1.48)	(10.41)***
DQUALITY	1.404	3.024	3.689
	(6.58)***	(9.69)***	(14.57)***
DAREA	0.418	–1.774	–1.249
	(1.85)*	–(4.47)***	–(4.21)***
DAREA1	–0.0851	–1.010	–0.749
	–(0.371)	–(3.22)***	–(2.74)**
DSEX	0.0943	–0.324	–0.113
	(0.573)	–(1.05)	–(0.46)
SIZFAMIL	–0.247	–0.199	–0.330
	–(5.88)***	–(1.70)*	–(4.09)***
DOCC	0.587	0.076	0.692
	(2.31)**	(0.17)	(2.13)**
DOCCI	0.0813	0.00754	0.0453
	(0.54)	(0.02)	(0.17)

LOG-LIKELIHOOD.. –1468.9
RESTRICTED (SLOPE = 0) LOG-L...–2438.1
CHI-SQUARE.. 1938.4
DEGREES OF FREEDOM.. 48

(Contd.)

$$\rho^2 = 1 - \frac{L^*(\beta)}{L^*(0)} = 1 - .60 = 0.40$$

PCP = 69.7

ACTUAL	TOTAL	PREDICTED 0	1	2	3	%
TOTAL	2058	818	826	45	369	
0	289	601	173	5	10	207.9
1	818	176	569	9	64	69.5
2	103	26	8	20	49	19.5
3	348	15	76	11	246	70.6

TABLE 6.9: Multinomial Logit Results for All Owners with Income Greater than 30.000 Cr.

Variable	Coeff (EQ 1) Larger House	Coeff (EQ 2) Smaller Apt.	Coeff (EQ 3) Larger Apt.
ASC	–8.49	–7.660	–7.44
	(3.01)	–(2.25)	–(2.60)
MONTHPAY	0.0000526	0.000110	0.000133
	(0.54)	(1.10)	(1.37)
INCDOMI	0.0000127	–0.0000690	0.0000115
	(1.25)	(0.63)	(1.13)
AGE	0.113	0.225	0.109
	(1.05)	(1.73)	(1.01)
AGESQ	–0.000813	–0.00219	–0.000908
	–(0.79)	–(1.73)	–(0.87)
DCOLOR	0.417	0.849	0.692
	(0.90)	(1.26)	(1.43)
DSCHOOL	0.602	1.749	1.419
	(0.75)	(1.93)*	(1.76)
DSCHOOL1	1.094	1.484	1.813
	(1.44)	(1.66)	(2.36)**
DSCHOOL2	0.0336	0.822	0.820
	(0.06)	(1.26)	(1.60)
NUBROOM	3.239	1.362	2.777
	(6.67)***	(2.43)**	(5.69)***
DQUALITY	1.405	2.761	3.582
	(2.37)**	(4.00)***	(6.04)***
DAREA	1.237	–1.693	–0.407
	(2.12)**	–(1.98)*	–(0.69)

(Contd)

TABLE 6.9 *(Contd.)*

Variable	Coeff (EQ 1) Larger House	Coeff (EQ 2) Smaller Apt.	Coeff (EQ 3) Larger Apt.
DAREA1	1.230	–0.508	0.0305
	(2.16)**	–(0.811)	(0.05)
DSEX	0.734	0.753	0.550
	(1.32)	(1.15)	(0.980)
SIZFAMIL	–0.506	–0.752	–0.563
	–(3.60)***	–(3.41)***	–(3.88)***
DOCC	0.584	0.664	0.832
	(1.02)	(1.02)	(1.44)
DOCCI	–0.317	–0.353	–0.336
	–(0.57)	–(0.479)	–(0.59)

LOG-LIKELIHOOD.. –886.95
RESTRICTED (SLOPE = 0) LOG-L...–1364.5
CHI-SQUARE... 955.3
DEGREES OF FREEDOM.. 48

$$\rho^2 = 1 - \frac{L^*(\beta)}{L^*(0)} = 1 - .65 = 0.35$$

PCP = 77.8

ACTUAL	TOTAL	PREDICTED 0	1	2	3	%
TOTAL	1551	26	446	1	1078	
0	39	14	19	0	6	35.9
1	501	4	334	1	162	66.6
2	58	4	4	0	50	0.0
3	953	4	89	0	860	90.2

Analysis of Households by Region

This section analyses the results of the multinomial logit model for all households. The exercise is intended to see if there are any regional variations in the household decision of choosing different dwelling units. Table 6.10 presents the results for low income regions, middle income regions are presented in Table 6.11, and high income regions are presented in Table 6.12. The monthly payment variable (MONTHPAY) is positive for all three equations but is insignificant for the larger house equation (Table 6.10). Low income households prefer larger houses and larger apartments to small houses if all other variables are held constant. We also find that they prefer smaller apartments to smaller houses. These results are not surprising since we would expect households to prefer larger units if they intend to pay more per month. In the middle income region the coefficient of monthly payment for a larger house has a negative coefficient and is also insignificant. Although the sign of the coefficient suggests that households in this region would prefer smaller houses to larger houses as the monthly payments rise, the results are not definitive as evidenced by the low *t*-value. It is clear, however, that household preference is toward apartments with stronger preference given for larger over smaller apartments. The coefficients for the apartments are highly significant. In the high income region (Table 6.12) the coefficient for monthly payment is positive and significant for all the equations. In this region households prefer larger houses and apartments as the payments rise. The decision-makers will also prefer to move into larger units within each category of house type.

Income of the household is an important determinant of housing choice especially in the middle income region (Table 6.11). Note that all the coefficients are positive and significant. As the income rises, households will choose larger units of housing. However, if they intend to choose smaller units, then they will prefer smaller apartments over smaller houses (the coefficient for small apartments being positive and significant). In the low and high income regions we find that all the income coefficients are positive, but are insignificant for smaller apartments. Thus, in these two regions we are uncertain about their preference between smaller houses and smaller apartments, but they prefer larger apartments over larger houses. (The coefficient for larger apartments is higher than the coefficient for larger houses). In summary, we could say that irrespective of the region all households will prefer a larger unit over a smaller unit if income and monthly payments rise. They may also prefer smaller apartments over smaller houses especially in the middle income region.

The variables measuring the impact of age on housing choice do not give us much insight since most of them are insignificant.

However, the only exception is in the low and high income regions where the coefficients are significant for smaller apartments. The AGESQ variable in general has a negative sign across all regions, suggesting that households will prefer smaller housing during later years of their lives. This will then help reduce the maintenance and upkeep costs of the unit. Only in the low income regions is this variable positive for the large apartments but is not significant.

There are some interesting results given by the variable (DCOLOR) Race. In all regions we find that white household heads are more likely to prefer larger units in general or smaller apartments over small houses. The value of the coefficients are also higher for larger apartments compared to larger houses, suggesting an inclination toward apartments over houses. In the middle income region, whites are more likely to choose larger units compared to the whites in the low income regions. (The coefficients in the middle income region are much greater and significant than in the low income regions). Table 6.12 suggests a different outcome. None of the coefficients (DCOLOR) are significant. The race of the household head does not explain to any degree housing choice in the high income region. Household heads who prefer to live in the high income regions are more likely to choose larger units of housing irrespective of their race.

The variable measuring the impact of the level of education of the household is very unpredictable. The results indicate that irrespective of the level of education and the region household prefer larger apartments over larger houses. The coefficients for larger apartments are positive and are significant. This result may be due to the fact that the head of the household indicated in the survey may not be the decision-maker in reality. In a country like Brazil where joint family systems exist, this is quite possible. Since the education variable measures the impact of education of the head of the household (generally the oldest person in the household). It may not explain the choice correctly. Thus, caution should be exercised in its interpretation.

Households who desire to have more bedrooms prefer a larger house or a larger apartment, thus will move between the same category, however, they would prefer smaller houses to small apartments. As indicated earlier this may be because there is a possibility of additions to smaller houses but not to smaller apartments. In general, the apartments are of superior quality compared to houses. Households who place importance to the quality of housing (measured by the material used in its construction) will tend to place a greater preference to apartments. This is consistent with the analysis of the results in previous sections.

The variable measuring the sex of the household head (DSEX) has all insignificant coefficients. Sex of the household head does not add much to the decision-making process. This is true across all regions. The family size variable (SIZFAMIL) is negative and is significant across all regions. This follows the same trend which was seen in Tables 6.1, 6.2 and 6.3. We only get some insight on this variable when household heads are classified into renters and owners, which has been explained earlier.

Households who are employed in administrative and professional occupations and who live in low income regions prefer larger houses and larger apartments. However, they choose smaller houses to smaller apartments (based on the sign of the coefficient). However, the coefficient for smaller apartments are insignificant, casting doubt on the result. In the middle income region, these households will prefer larger houses over larger apartments. Their preference is toward larger houses compared to larger apartments. In the high income regions (Table 6.12) the variable measuring the impact of occupation is negative and insignificant for all the equations. Thus, no concrete evidence is found to make any positive statements. Again, this may be due to the explanation given in the case of the educational variable, that the household head may not be the actual decision-maker in the high income regions.

Overall the model performs well for all regions. As indicated by the log likelihood ratio of 0.36 for low income regions, 0.40 for middle income regions, and 0.43 for high income regions. The percentages correctly predicated are high enough to state that the model is good. The model performs better for the low income region and the high income region with PCP being 71.0 and 74.8, respectively. In the low income region the model predicts best for houses, 78.4 per cent for small houses and 75.5 for larger houses. It predicts very badly for small apartments (5.6%), but the sample is very small. In the middle and high income regions the model predicts best for smaller houses and larger apartments – 76.9 per cent and 81.5 per cent and 77.3 per cent and 87.2 per cent, respectively).

TABLE 6.10: **Multinomial Logit Results for All Households in the Low Income Region**

Variable	Coeff (EQ 1) Larger House	Coeff (EQ 2) Smaller Apt.	Coeff (EQ 3) Larger Apt.
ASC	–6.277	–6.242	–7.542
	–(8.931)	–(3.44)	–(6.85)
MONTHPAY	.0000525	.000271	0.000236
	(1.34)	(4.29)***	(5.31)***
INCDOMI	.0000405	.00000690	.0000498
	(5.93)***	(0.43)	(6.52)***
AGE	.0535	0.184	–0.00192
	(1.87)*	(2.24)**	–(0.04)
AGESQ	–.000308	–.00211	0.000302
	– (1.06)	(2.23)**	(0.69)
DCOLOR	0.451	0.636	0.731
	(3.28)***	(2.01)**	(3.24)**
DSCHOOL	–0.556	–0.273	1.041
	(1.16)	(0.31)	(1.84)*
DSCHOOL1	0.248	0.241	0.956
	–(0.09)	(0.49)	(2.74)**
DSCHOOL2	0.125	–0.0191	0.877
	(0.71)	–(0.04)	(3.18)***
NUBROOM	2.374	–0.0770	2.475
	(16.01)***	–(0.19)	(12.26)***
DQUALITY	1.103	2.097	3.162
	(4.68)***	(5.70)***	(11.70)***
DSEX	0.303	0.203	–2.268
	(1.62)	(0.50)	(0.92)
SIZFAMIL	–0.224	–0.349	–0.437
	–(4.93)***	–(2.58)**	–(5.24)***
DOCC	0.528	–0.0707	0.769
	(2.34)**	(0.16)	(2.56)**
DOCC1	–0.144	–1.044	–0.00552
	–(0.89)	–(2.35)**	–(0.02)

LOG-LIKELIHOOD .... –1264.6
RESTRICTED (SLOPE = 0) LOG-L........................ –1962.8
CHI-SQUARE.. 1396.5
DEGREES OF FREEDOM.. 42

$$\rho^2 = 1 - \frac{L^*(\beta)}{L^*(0)} = 1 - .65 = 0.35$$

PCP = 71.0

Contd.)

		PREDICTED				
ACTUAL	TOTAL	0	1	2	3	%
TOTAL	1820	804	870	9	137	.
0	767	602	154	1	6	78.4
1	794	160	600	1	33	75.5
2	53	33	8	3	9	5.6
3	210	9	108	4	89	42.2

TABLE 6.11: Multinomial Logit Results for All Households in Middle Income Region

Variable	Coeff (EQ 1) Larger House	Coeff (EQ 2) Smaller Apt.	Coeff (EQ 3) Larger Apt.
ASC	–6.92	–3.024	–9.323
	–(9.74)	–(3.59)	–(11.21)
MONTHPAY	–0.0000320	0.0000715	0.0000951
	–(1.12)	(2.29)**	(3.35)***
INCDOMI	0.0000454	.0000318	0.0000451
	(7.94)***	(4.85)**	(7.67)***
AGE	0.0474	0.0510	0.0888
	(1.65)	(1.40)	(2.70)**
AGESQ	–0.000148	–0.000537	–0.000549
	–(0.51)	(1.42)	–(1.67)
DCOLOR	0.837	0.549	1.278
	(5.84)**	(2.89)**	(7.00)***
DSCHOOL	0.491	0.465	1.392
	(1.44)	(1.22)	(4.03)***
DSCHOOL1	0.361	0.218	0.958
	(1.52)	(0.77)	(3.85)***
DSCHOOL2	–0.00754	0.261	0.533
	–(0.04)	(1.18)	(2.68)***
NUBROOM	2.246	–0.335	1.835
	(15.70)***	–(1.57)	(11.87)***
DQUALITY	0.747	2.343	3.164
	(4.25)***	(12.27)***	(17.30)***
DSEX	0.219	–0.229	0.0625
	(1.29)	–(1.09)	(0.32)
SIZFAMIL	–0.506	–0.752	–0.563
	–(3.60)***	–(3.41)***	–(3.88)***
DOCC	–0.205	–0.257	–0.255
	–(4.18)***	–(3.31)***	(4.18)***
DOCC1	0.180	–0.0158	0.222
	(1.11)	–(0.07)	(1.14)

(Contd.)

LOG-LIKELIHOOD	–2182.8
RESTRICTED (SLOPE = 0) LOG-L	–3593.9
CHI-SQUARE	2822.1
DEGREES OF FREEDOM	42

$$\rho^2 = 1 - \frac{L^*(\beta)}{L^*(0)} = 1 - .60 = 0.40$$

PCP = 66.5

		PREDICTED				
ACTUAL	TOTAL	0	1	2	3	%
TOTAL	2762	864	668	141	1089	
0	782	602	110	33	37	67.9
1	824	160	437	14	213	53.0
2	250	82	7	61	100	24.4
3	906	20	114	33	739	81.5

TABLE 6.12: Multinomial Logit Results for All Households in High Income Region

Variable	Coeff (EQ 1) Larger House	Coeff (EQ 2) Smaller Apt.	Coeff (EQ 3) Larger Apt.
ASC	–7.251	–3.833	–7.480
	–(5.59)	–(2.95)	–(5.98)
MONTHPAY	0.000251	0.000316	0.000308
	(2.99)**	(3.77)***	(3.69)***
INCDOMI	0.0000198	0.00000938	0.0000244
	(2.07)**	(0.96)	(2.56)***
AGE	0.102	0.169	0.0771
	(1.92)*	(3.31)***	(1.48)
AGESQ	–0.000668	–0.00173	–0.000494
	–(1.25)	–(3.28)***	–(0.94)
DCOLOR	0.216	0.00523	0.301
	(0.72)	(0.02)	(1.00)
DSCHOOL	1.983	2.519	3.382
	(1.70)	(2.19)**	(2.93)**
DSCHOOL1	0.111	0.475	1.265
	(0.20)	(0.94)	(2.46)**
DSCHOOL2	0.380	0.554	1.418
	(1.09)	(1.68)	(4.18)
NUBROOM	2.171	–0.701	1.162
	(7.25)***	(2.19)**	(5.59)***
DQUALITY	1.165	3.168	3.968
	(3.04)***	(8.80)***	(10.31)***

(Contd)

TABLE 6.12 *(Contd.)*

Variable	Coeff (EQ 1) Larger House	Coeff (EQ 2) Smaller Apt.	Coeff (EQ 3) Larger Apt.
DSEX	0.664	0.327	0.357
	(1.84)	(0.99)	(1.04)
SIZFAMIL	–0.332	–0.324	–0.222
	–(3.15)***	–(3.30)***	–(2.26)***
DOCC	–0.208	–0.697	–0.522
	–(0.44)	–(1.52)	–(1.15)
DOCC1	–0.00665	–0.234	–0.121
	–(0.02)	–(0.73)	–(0.34)

LOG-LIKELIHOOD..	– 1030.9
RESTRICTED (SLOPE = 0) LOG-L..........................	–1803.7
CHI-SQUARE..	1545.7
DEGREES OF FREEDOM......................................	42

$$\rho^2 = 1 - \frac{L^*(\beta)}{L^*(0)} = 1 - .58 = 0.43$$

PCP = 74.8

		PREDICTED				
ACTUAL	TOTAL	0	1	2	3	%
TOTAL	1585	192	123	310	960	
0	163	126	18	14	5	77.3
1	199	24	73	14	88	36.6
2	320	39	3	199	79	62.1
3	903	3	29	83	788	87.2

Derivatives of Choice Probabilities and Elasticities

In a choice model as we have estimated, the choice probabilities are a function of observed variables. It is often useful to know the extent to which these probabilities change in response to a change in some observed variable. for example, it would be of interest to know by how much the probability of choosing a particular type of dwelling unit changes due to a change in the number of rooms.

To address these types of questions, derivatives of the choice probabilities have to be calculated. The change in the probability of choosing alternative *i* given a change in an observed factor Y_{in} entering the representative utility of alternative *i* and holding the representative utility of other alternatives constant can be derived for a multinomial case as follows:

$$P_{in} = \frac{e^{X\beta_i}}{1+\sum_2^J e^{X\beta_i}} \quad i = 1 \ldots\ldots J$$

$$\frac{\partial P_i}{\partial X_k} = \frac{\beta_{ik} e^{x\beta_i}\left(1+\sum_2^J e^{x\beta_i}\right) - e^{x\beta_i} \cdot \sum_2^J \beta_{jk} e^{x\beta j}}{\left(1+\sum_2^J e^{x\beta j}\right)^2}$$

$$\frac{\partial P_i}{\partial X_k} = \beta_{ik} \frac{e^{X\beta_i}}{1+\sum_2^J e^{X\beta_j}} - p_i \sum_2^J \beta_{kj} P_j$$

$$\frac{\partial P_i}{\partial X_k} = B_{ik} P_i - P_i(\beta_{ik} - \sum_2^J \beta_{jk} P_j$$

$$\frac{\partial P_i}{\partial X_k} = P_i\left(\beta_{ik} - \sum_2^J \beta_{jk} P_j\right)$$

Although derivations give us the rate of change, they are not easy to interpret. Economists often measure response by elasticities rather than derivatives: since elasticities are normalized for the variable units. As elasticity is the percentage change in one variable that is associated with a percentage change in another variable. The elasticity of P_{in} with respect to X_{in}' a variable entering the utility if alternative *i* is given by:

$$e_{ix} = (\delta P_i/\delta X_k)\,(X_k/P_i)$$

In order to explain the extent of variation in the probability of choosing a specific type of dwelling we make use of the elasticity concept developed in the preceding pages. Tables 6.13, 6.14, and 6.15 present the derivatives of choice probabilities and the relevant elasticities for all households, low income households, and high income households, respectively. Table 6.13 indicates that if monthly payments rise by one per cent then the probability of choosing a larger house in relation to a smaller house rises by about half a percent. This elasticity is greater than that for large apartments, which is only 0.21 per cent. The increase in the probability of choosing a smaller apartment is 0.89 per cent which is higher than for both larger houses and larger apartments. This is due to the fact that households will be more likely to substitute a smaller apartment when the monthly payment rises. They may tend to move into apartment which are located in better areas compared to their present dwelling. It would be much more difficult for households to more into larger units.

TABLE 6.13: Derivatives and Elasticities for All Households

Variable	Larger House	Smaller Apt.	Larger Apt.
Derivatives of Choice Probabilities			
Monthpay	0.0000844	0.000114	0.0000516
Income	–0.0000233	0.0000124	0.00000461
Age	–0.0227	0.0586	–0.0120
Nubroom	0.510	–0.498	0.588
Sizfamil	0.0762	–0.178	–0.0120
Elasticity Measures			
Monthpay	0.46	0.89	0.21
Income	–0.156	1.20	0.23
Age	–1.72	6.46	–0.67
Nubroom	1.60	–2.27	1.37
Sizfamil	0.44	–1.49	–0.05

Note: Elasticities have been calculated at the mean.

The income elasticity is highest for smaller apartments. This reinforces what the author has been said earlier that households may prefer the same size of a dwelling in better locations if rents were to rise, the same reasoning holds true for income. We also find that a one per cent increase in income increases the probability of choosing a larger apartment by 0.23 per cent but decreases the probability of choosing a larger house by 0.156 indicating that as incomes rise households will prefer apartments over houses.

The elasticity value of the number of bedrooms for larger houses and larger apartments are very high, and we would expect this result. A one per cent increase in the number of bedrooms increases the probability of choosing a larger house by 1.60 per cent and 1.37 per cent for larger apartments. Households will make a switch to larger units as the size of the unit changes by a small amount, given that all other factors are held constant. The NUBROOM has a negative elasticity for smaller apartments indicating that a one per cent increase in the number of bedrooms will decrease the probability of choosing a smaller apartment by 2.27 per cent. Thus this indicates that households will prefer a smaller house to a smaller apartment. This is due to the fact that houses have more open space available although it may be of the same size in terms of the floor space.

The analysis in the previous section has indicated a negative coefficient for the size of the family. However when we calculated the elasticities for the size of the family we find that the family size elasticity for larger houses is positive indicating that households will prefer larger houses if the size of the family increases. A one per cent increase in the size of the family increases the probability of choosing a larger house by about half a per cent; however the probability of choosing a smaller apartment falls by about one and half per cent. The elasticity for larger apartments is too small for any interpretation. However, it helps to evaluate its sign which is negative. What these results indicate is that there is an increase in the probability of choosing a house but a decline in the probability of choosing an apartment as family size increases. This result is also consistent across all income groups (Tables 6.14 and 6.15). In general households prefer houses over apartments as family size rises. This result does not agree with the finding of Table 6.24, where elasticities are repeated for all households in high income regions. The table indicates that size of the family elasticity in this region is positive for larger houses and larger apartments. A one per cent increase in the size of the family increases the probability of choosing a larger house by 0.19 per cent and by 0.31 per cent for larger apartments; but decreases by 0.12 per cent for smaller apartments. This suggests that households who live in high income regions will prefer larger houses provided they are not located in less preferable areas.

TABLE 6.14: Derivatives and Elasticities for Low Income Households

Variable	Larger House	Smaller Apt.	Larger Apt.
Derivatives of Choice Probabilities			
Monthpay	–0.000110	0.000171	0.0000415
Income	–0.00000974	0.0000218	0.00000218
Age	–0.00550	0.0541	–0.0386
Nubroom	0.681	–0.747	0.595
Sizfamil	0.0898	–0.232	–0.0198
Elasticity Measures			
Monthpay	–0.28	0.56	0.10
Income	–0.23	0.68	0.53
Age	–0.41	5.21	–2.48
Nubroom	1.84	–0.26	1.59
Sizfamil	0.51	–1.92	–0.11

Note: Elasticities have been calculated at the mean.

TABLE 6.15: Derivatives and Elasticities for High Income Households

Variable	Larger House	Smaller Apt.	Larger Apt.
Derivatives of Choice Probabilities			
Monthpay	–0.0000582	0.0000498	0.0000584
Income	0.000000307	0.00000285	0.00000474
Age	–0.0152	0.0268	0.0143
Nubroom	0.446	–0.172	0.458
Sizfamil	0.0410	–0.0829	–0.803
Elasticity Measures			
Monthpay	–0.55	1.16	0.39
Income	0.04	0.89	0.42
Age	–1.15	0.78	0.74
Nubroom	1.58	–1.57	1.19
Sizfamil	0.24	–1.18	–0.33

Note: Elasticities have been calculated at the mean.

Table 6.14, indicates the elasticities for low income households. Some interesting patterns emerge. The monthly payments and income elasticities indicate that even for this group of households the probability of choosing a smaller apartment or a larger apartment rises with increases in monthly payments or household incomes. We also find that a one per cent increase in monthly payments and/or income decreases the probability of choosing a larger house by 0.28 per cent and 0.23 per cent respectively. This suggests that low income households will substitute larger housing for smaller housing in preferable areas. All the other variables show a similar trend as is indicated in Table 6.13 for all households.

Table 6.15 presents the results for high income households. A one per cent increase in income increases the probability of choosing a larger house by 0.04 per cent, by 0.42 for larger apartments, and 0.89 for smaller apartments in relation to the smaller house. In all the tables we find a similar trend for the number of rooms. An increase in the number of rooms increases the probability of choosing a larger unit irrespective of the income group or the regional groupings.

Comparison of all renters and all owners provides us with some clues to the variation in the decision-making process. There is an increase in the probability of owning a larger house or apartment as monthly payments rise (Table 6.19). However, the same is not true to the renters. Renters are less likely to choose a larger house as monthly payments rise. The probability of choosing a smaller apartments or a larger apartment rises indicating that apartments in general are preferable to houses. The owners also have a positive income elasticity for all the three types of housing. The probability of choosing a larger house and an apartment rises as income rises.

TABLE 6.16: Multinomial Logit Results for All Renters

Variable	Larger House	Smaller Apt.	Larger Apt.
Derivatives of Choice Probabilities			
Monthpay	–0.0000679	0.000198	0.0000903
Income	–0.00000612	0.0000236	0.00000392
Age	–0.0176	0.0785	–0.0247
Nubroom	0.498	0.326	0.459
Sizfamil	0.0811	–0.0272	0.0161
Elasticity Measures			
Monthpay	–0.77	1.72	0.58
Income	–0.44	1.31	0.16
Age	–1.64	0.56	–1.31
Nubroom	1.84	–0.92	0.96
Sizfamil	0.57	–1.47	0.06

Note: Elasticities have been calculated at the mean.

TABLE 6.17: Derivatives and Elasticities for Low Income Renters

Variable	Larger House	Smaller Apt.	Larger Apt.
Derivatives of Choice Probabilities			
Monthpay	–0.0000339	0.000162	0.0000751
Income	–0.0000107	0.0000246	0.0000372
Age	–0.00989	0.0844	–0.0463
Nubroom	0.495	–0.652	0.773
Sizfamil	0.108	–0.381	–0.0468
Elasticity Measures			
Monthpay	–0.28	0.83	0.33
Income	–0.52	0.66	0.80
Age	–1.13	0.63	–0.81
Nubroom	1.95	1.89	1.62
Sizfamil	0.90	–1.94	–0.20

Note: Elasticities have been calculated at the mean.

TABLE 6.18: Derivatives and Elasticites for High Income Renters

Variable	Larger House	Smaller Apt.	Larger Apt.
Derivatives of Choice Probabilities			
Monthpay	–0.000138	0.000308	0.0000396
Income	–0.00000434	0.0000227	–0.00000898
Age	–0.00260	–0.00954	0.0154
Nubroom	0.818	–0.682	0.654
Sizfamil	–0.0280	0.0487	–0.0412
Elasticity Measures			
Monthpay	–2.08	1.04	0.39
Income	–4.85	2.46	–0.70
Age	–0.19	–0.66	0.77
Nubroom	2.83	–2.29	1.59
Sizfamil	–0.16	0.27	–0.17

Note: Elasticities have been calculated at the mean.

TABLE 6.19: Derivatives and Elasticities for All Owners

Variable	Larger House	Smaller Apt.	Larger Apt.
Derivatives of Choice Probabilities			
Monthpay	–0.0000644	0.0000300	0.000153
Income	0.00000312	0.00000146	0.00000861
Age	0.000415	0.0109	0.00175
Nubroom	0.433	–0.0445	0.322
Sizfamil	0.00941	–0.0196	–0.0886
Elasticity Measures			
Monthpay	0.18	0.86	0.36
Income	0.21	0.98	0.47
Age	0.03	1.73	0.10
Nubroom	1.33	–1.34	0.79
Sizfamil	0.05	1.07	–0.39

Note: Elasticities have been calculated at the mean.

TABLE 6.20: Derivatives and Elasticities for Low Income Owners

Variable	Larger House	Smaller Apt.	Larger Apt.
Derivatives of Choice Probabilities			
Monthpay	–0.000408	0.000259	0.000422
Income	–0.0000134	0.0000143	0.0000467
Age	0.0201	0.0219	–0.0524
Nubroom	0.593	–0.259	0.412
Sizfamil	0.0170	–0.0433	–0.0847
Elasticity Measures			
Monthpay	–0.18	0.42	0.19
Income	–0.28	1.07	0.97
Age	1.36	1.62	1.69
Nubroom	1.50	–1.23	1.02
Sizfamil	0.09	0.83	–0.44

Note: Elasticities have been calculated at the mean.

TABLE 6.21: Derivatives and Elasticities for High Income Owners

Variable	Larger House	Smaller Apt.	Larger Apt.
Derivatives of Choice Probabilities			
Monthpay	–0.0000448	0.00	0.0000883
Income	0.00000155	0.00	0.00000274
Age	0.00977	0.00	0.0304
Nubroom	0.488	0.00	0.559
Sizfamil	0.00121	0.00	–0.203
Elasticity Measures			
Monthpay	–0.27	–	0.40
Income	0.20	–	0.26
Age	0.73	–	1.66
Nubroom	1.80	–	1.52
Sizfamil	0.006	–	–0.83

Note: Elasticities have been calculated at the mean.

TABLE 6.22: Derivatives and Elasticities for Low Income Regions

Variable	Larger House	Smaller Apt.	Larger Apt.
Derivatives of Choice Probabilities			
Monthpay	–0.0000471	0.0000186	0.0000766
Income	0.0000143	–0.000000680	0.00000796
Age	0.0322	0.00783	–0.0223
Nubroom	0.629	–0.0788	0.290
Sizfamil	–0.0148	–0.0184	–0.105
Elasticity Measures			
Monthpay	–0.09	0.48	0.26
Income	0.41	–0.26	0.41
Age	1.92	1.13	–1.13
Nubroom	1.49	–1.16	1.13
Sizfamil	–0.08	–1.26	–0.95

Note: Elasticities have been calculated at the mean.

The results when evaluated at the regional level provides us with some insights of variation between regions. We find that in the high income regions the households are relatively inelastic to changes in monthly payments in the larger apartments. However, there seems to be more variation in the probabilities to changes in income. Households are also very sensitive to changes in the dwelling size in this region. In the middle income region households also are relatively sensitive to changes in dwelling size compared to households in low income regions. The age elasticity fluctuates from one group to the other and from one region to the other. However, we find that the absolute elasticity values are quite high. Table 6.22 indicates that in low income regions as the households grow older the probability of choosing a larger apartment falls which conforms with the behavior in the high income region. This trend does not exist in the middle income region. Overall, the elasticity measures have given us further details and insights into the decision-making process.

TABLE 6.23: Derivatives and Elasticities for Middle Income Regions

Variable	Larger House	Smaller Apt.	Larger Apt.
Derivatives of Choice Probabilities			
Monthpay	–0.0000672	0.0000484	0.0000771
Income	0.000000468	0.00000754	0.0000108
Age	–0.0198	0.0215	0.0417
Nubroom	0.461	–0.284	0.591
Sizfamil	0.0347	–0.0786	–0.0681
Elasticity Measures			
Monthpay	–0.35	0.55	0.27
Income	0.33	1.16	0.49
Age	–1.72	1.89	2.36
Nubroom	1.58	–2.21	1.37
Sizfamil	0.22	–1.11	–0.29

Note: Elasticities have been calculated at the mean.

TABLE 6.24: Derivatives and Elasticities for High Income Regions

Variable	Larger House	Smaller Apt.	Larger Apt.
Derivatives of Choice Probabilities			
Monthpay	–0.0000782	0.000329	0.0000173
Income	–0.00000267	0.0000103	0.00000986
Age	–0.0256	0.148	–0.0568
Nubroom	0.583	–0.424	0.699
Sizfamil	0.0229	–0.240	0.0878
Elasticity Measures			
Monthpay	–1.30	0.32	0.12
Income	–0.48	0.36	0.75
Age	–1.25	1.17	–1.03
Nubroom	2.30	–1.36	1.60
Sizfamil	0.19	–0.12	0.31

Note: Elasticities have been calculated at the mean.

7

POLICY IMPLICATIONS

Overview

This chapter presents the methodological, theoretical, and policy contribution of this study. There has been a historical progression towards incorporating variables that permit greater behavioral realism in housing choice studies. Urban economists, for example, have expanded the traditional approach to housing choice by incorporating environmental and neighborhood externalities (Richardson, 1977), varying consumer tastes (Backman, 1974), and residential neighborhood attractiveness (Papageorgiou, 1976). This study fits into this scheme of incorporating behavioural variables by examining housing choice patterns by several income and demographic subscales within and between housing submarkets in urban Rio.

Microeconomic analysis of housing demand have two major characteristics. They are aggregate in nature and have tried to draw parallels between developed and developing countries. Urban economists have tried to address the issue of aggregation, by incorporating submarkets into their analysis, however, they have failed to look at the variation in household choice process within these submarkets. Comparative studies of developed and developing countries (Houlhakker, 1965; Mayo, 1981) have found some commonalities; however, there is a great deal of variation in the choice process when socially and culturally determined variables such as household size and age of the head have been incorporated. Some studies (Leeds, 1974; Perlman, 1976) have drawn attention to the differences in household behaviour, relative to western economies. These differences result from the socio-cultural, demographic, and economic variables that reflect the Latin American culture in general, and the Cariola culture of Rio specifically. This section therefore will also highlight the commonalities and the differences in the housing choice behavior patterns in Rio and those in developed countries.

Income is not treated as an aggregate variable, as it is in the case of most housing choice studies. In this study housing choice patterns of households are examined, within the context of their variations across income groups. This is in line with studies (Lakshmanan, 1978) that emphasize the variations in income elasticity with levels of income. The major findings and theoretical contributions pertaining to the study are summarized below. The policy implications of the findings are then highlighted, followed by a discussion of future research directions.

Effect of Household Attributes on Housing Choice

Multinomial logit analysis indicates a strong and highly significant relationship between household income and the housing type predicted by the model. Our results indicate that irrespective of which income group a person belongs to, he will have a tendency to opt for larger units of housing within the group with an increase in income. As his income rises, there is however, evidence to suggest that low income households will prefer smaller houses over smaller apartments. This suggests preference for more open space and a possibility of future expansion of the unit, which is not possible in the case of apartments. Analysis conducted on renters and owners indicated that renters overall have a preference for larger dwellings as incomes rise. We also find that renters as a group have a greater tendency to live in larger apartments over larger houses, but the same is not true when renters are classified by income groups. It was found that high income renters show a greater preference for larger houses over larger apartments. An analysis of owner groups showed results indicating a higher probability of choosing a larger unit over smaller unit as incomes rise. However, there is substantial variation in the values of the coefficients when renters are viewed as belonging to different income groups. Our analysis of low income owners suggests that, they will prefer to own larger apartments over larger houses and larger houses over smaller houses. There is also evidence that high income owners prefer larger apartments over larger houses, but they prefer smaller houses over smaller apartments.

Our analysis has provided a clear-cut evidence of the link between household income and choice of housing type. Overall, we find that irrespective of the income group that a household belongs to they prefer larger apartments and larger houses as income rises. There is also evidence to suggest that their preference is more toward larger apartments compared to larger houses. These results contradict the results of the studies conducted in Western countries where it was found that as household incomes rise, households tend to choose larger houses over larger apartments (Axel Borsch-Supan, 1987). However, it is not possible to generalize this trend for all developing countries. Rio, due to its location on the ocean coast may exhibit trends which may not be true in other developing countries. Most apartments in Rio are located on the ocean front, which makes it more attractive to households, since these are also the area with most public utility services, thus, Households will be attracted to this location.

Another important finding which is also supported by studies in developed countries is the importance of the life cycle variable. It is found that households have a tendency to choose smaller units of housing as they enter the retirement age. It was also found that as households age overtime they prefer apartments in general or larger houses. However, our analysis did not find support to this trend when we viewed household within different income groups. Households with low incomes showed a tendency to prefer relatively larger houses and relatively smaller apartments. However, the high income households showed a tendency to prefer apartments or relatively larger houses. Overall, our analysis of the preference with respect to age indicates that in general low income households live in houses and high income households in apartments. This result is again contrary to the results of studies done in developed countries like the United States and West Germany where the rich prefer houses and the poor prefer apartments.

An analysis of the life cycle variable for the renter group and the owner group, showed some differences in the choice process. Over the life cycle, high income owner household do not prefer smaller houses, they continue to show an inclination towards larger apartments in general. In the case of renter groups, the coefficient was statistically insignificant. Thus, we cannot make any conclusive remarks.

Another important variable that determines housing choice in our study is the level of education of the head of the household. When households are taken as a group we find that as the educational level of the head of the household increases, households in general show a stronger preference for larger units. There is also evidence to suggest that among the high income households, those with higher levels of education prefer larger apartments over larger house. In fact, apartments are preferred over houses for all levels of education. Renters as a group are more likely to choose a larger dwelling if they have twelve or more years of schooling. They also tend to prefer larger apartments over larger houses. There is also evidence to suggest that renters would prefer a smaller house over smaller apartments as the level of education increases. When we conducted an analysis of low income renters we found that all the coefficients were insignificant, indicating that level of education may not play a major role in housing choice decisions for low income renters. The study also found evidence to suggest that irrespective of the level of education high income renters prefer larger houses and any size apartments over small houses. Owners, on the other hand, were found to show greater preference for apartments as the level of education rises.

The study also provided sufficient evidence indicating that white household heads are more likely to choose larger units compared to other races regardless of the income group. Similar trends were found across income groups. This result is supported by most studies in developing countries (Goodman and Kawai, 1982; Henderson and Ioamides, 1983).

We also found that the occupation of the head of the household is an important predictor of housing choice. Our results indicate that household heads employed in professional and administrative occupations are more likely to choose larger units with a preference for apartments over houses. Low income renters show an inclination for houses over apartments in the same occupational group.

The most striking results in our study are those related to the size of the family. Studies conducted in developed countries suggest that as the size of the family increases, households will consume more housing space or choose to prefer larger units of housing. Our results do not show this trend. We found that all the coefficients for the size of the family have a negative sign; suggesting that as the size of the family increase, households will choose smaller units of housing. Our findings are supported by studies on Latin America (Samuel Aryeetey-Attoh, 1983) which found the family size elasticity to be negative. Studies conducted by Koth, Silva, and Dietz on housing in Latin America have suggested inflation as being the factor that causes this variable to be negative.

Effect of Dwelling Attributes on Housing Choice

The effects of the dwelling attitudes on housing choice are measured by the variable, NUBROOM and DQUALITY. We find that as the desire of the households to have more bedrooms increase, they will choose a larger unit of dwelling, wither larger houses or larger apartments. Their preference is greater for larger house compared to larger apartments. Our analysis also suggests that those households who prefer more bedrooms will choose smaller houses over smaller apartments. The impact of the NUBROOM across income groups suggests that households will prefer larger units of housing apartments in general. These households also prefer larger houses over larger apartments. The low income households however, prefer larger units of dwelling but in the case of smaller units they prefer smaller houses over smaller apartments. This trend is similar to the behavior of all renter groups and all owner groups. In general, renters and owners have similar preferences for the choice bases on the number of bedrooms.

Households who consider quality of housing to be important in the choice process prefer apartments over houses. This has also been true when households are classified by income groups. No evidence would be found from the studies in developed countries to either support or refute this result. However, we expect this result to hold for developed countries also, as in general apartment structures are made up of more durable materials. Similar trends were also found when households were classified as renters and owners.

The impact of locational variables measured by DAREA and DAREA1 are clear. Household who live in low and middle income areas prefer smaller units of housing or houses which are larger. This trend is seen across all income groups and also across renters and owners. Households who live in low income areas will choose houses over apartments.

Performance of the Modal

In conclusion, we would like to evaluate the overall performance of the model. We find that overall our model performs fairly well. The overall predictional range between 67 per cent to 81 per cent. The model predicts best for the high income groups. Overall, within the different types of dwelling, the model predicts best for smaller houses and larger apartments for all households. The same trend is found for the renter households and owner households.

Policy Implications

The major findings of this study have implications for strategic planning and effective project design for housing in Brazil. It should, however, be made clear that the policy evaluations of this section are extremely limited in scope. First it considers only the choice probabilities of individual households, not the aggregate group response. Farther, it is only a demand analysis in which the sample households may adjust all their choices rather than simply one or two aspects of it. For these reasons the impacts predicted should not be viewed as a resolution of a stable market equilibrium. For example, if due to a given policy the expected property taxes in low income regions were to decrease, the real-world short run impact may be an increase in housing price in the area. In the long run, new housing construction might be expected in the area. These changes will produce shifts in the demographic characteristics in the region, which in turn will alter household choice preferences. In short, the final collective reaction to a policy is determined by a robust process which is far more complex than the choice forecasts presented here indicate, and all conclusions drawn from the analysis should be viewed as preliminary in nature.

Any housing project in Rio should concentrate on providing smaller units of housing in preferable locations. This is supported by our most interesting finding, that as the household size increases, households will prefer smaller units of housing; our results indicate, that housing projects which add more space to what households already consumed would be more beneficial to the average small household than an average larger household. Since urban Rio has a larger proportion of larger households than smaller households, any policy which does not take this fact into account will fail to realize its goals.

It can also be suggested that any policy design should consider the different income groups of the target population, since choice behavior of households differ by income group.

Renters in Rio show an increased willingness to pay for an additional room as income increase. For these households, consider a project that increased the number of rooms designed by the policy maker. If the target beneficiary population varied by income, the benefits of such a project would be regressive.

We can also draw some policy conclusions on the structural quality of the dwellings. There is an indication that high income households prefer better dwelling quality. This indicates trading off increased size for greater structural quality and increased urban services would benefit a richer household more than a poorer household.

Another major public issue arises if we attempt to determine the distributional implications for providing certain packages of services. This is a concern especially for slum upgrading projects, where individual households do not apply to be project beneficiary but are chosen by neighborhood to be the subject of on-site development. Given the relatively wide mix of household types who are likely to be included in such a project, it becomes important to trace the distribution of benefits. Consider, for example two projects A and B which cost the same. Project A provides smaller dwellings but higher levels of structural quality and urban services than Project B. According to our results, the benefits of Project A would be regressive – the richer households among the recipient would benefit more than poorer households. Thus, the policy maker should be aware, that lower income households place greater priority on space relative to quality and the level of public services.

Finally, it seems important to emphasize on a more general level the strong evidence from this study that household behavior in the housing market is not erratic, but carefully considered. We have seen that different households behave in different ways thus leading to different choices. Not taking into account these behavioural differences in the choice process will have consequences that will defeat the fundamental goals of planners and project alike.

Also if policy-makers are to meet the needs of households they must pay attention to identifying the effective demand for housing and plan in a way consistent with that demand. The information on housing choice from this study can shift the planners focus in identifying housing production targets and standards, and in developing policies towards the building material industry and various housing system that can be afforded by different income groups.

Although we have made some policy recommendations based on the study, it is also advisable for us to review the current policies in Rio and try to suggest some alternative policy prescriptions keeping in view the drawbacks of the current policies in the face of the existing problems.

The inability of low income families and in many cases the middle income families to secure decent housing is the most immediate problem in urban Rio. Most policy-makers acknowledge that a satisfactory solution to this problem depends as much on the raising of income and standards of living as upon the building of new houses. The housing problem has become acute in the past decade due to walloping influx of migrants in the city of Rio.

In the past Rio has introduced a number of programmes of urban public housing. The basic unsolved problem is that the income of a high proportion of the urban families are too low to permit them to pay the cost of dwellings, that meet generally acceptable standards, while the government cannot afford to allocate enough funds to the housing agencies to provide heavily subsidized housing on a larger scale.

With a very few exceptions the housing agencies have not tried to meet this demand by lowering the standards and the cost of their dwelling units closer to the ability to pay of the poor; and they have made only a few small-scale experiments in urban aided self-help housing. There have also been few attempts by housing agencies to determine realistically what the city can afford to spend on housing and what relationship housing programs should have to other forms of public investment.

The consequence, has been that the neediest part of the city population has received practically no benefit from public housing programmes. Most of these programmes have been aimed at families with income falling within a range of permitting them to amortize the cost of housing over a period of 15 of 20 years. This group has included the lower middle class, the white collar employees, and civil servants. The housing programs have helped such families to escape from the slums, but they do not appreciably reduce the slum problem. Some of the current housing projects have involved the demolition of shanty-towns, but they have had the tendency of coming up in other places.

In Rio the policy of housing allotments has failed badly. Applicants for public housing are several times as numerous as the new dwelling units, the housing agencies have generally been able to select their tenants not only within a given income range, but also by the criteria of acceptable ways of life. The fact that the families are rarely selected on the basis of greatest need has meant that some problems that have become acute in the United Stated, in particular, have not yet become prominent. A policy of limiting low cost public housing to the neediest families can result in a kind of negative selection that prevents the development of acceptable ways of life in housing projects, Today the policy makers in Rio are troubled by a contradiction between the desirability of giving priority to the neediest in the allocation of limited public housing funds and the desirability of fostering balanced and stable neighborhoods.

On the basis of the study and the policies currently being used in Rio we have tried to make some additional policy recommendations which may be useful in improving the housing situation in Rio. We draw the attention of the policy-makers along the following lines:

1. Assistance and guidance should be given to families that build homes around the outskirts of the city. At present, while officially-sponsored self-help projects are rare, there is a great deal of unregulated building by workers who want something more than shacks. These workers, who have little capital to buy land and building materials, are often exploited by speculators who sell tiny plots of land without any provision of paved streets, water supplies, sewers, etc.
2. The municipality of the housing agencies should have alternate powers to prevent unauthorised shack buildings. At the same time it may be suggested that the most practical course is to permit the house builder to erect a temporary shack on his plot, then build a more substantial house as his time and ability to buy materials permit. The main drawback is that the first-comer, once be moves into his permanent house, will try to rent the temporary shack rather than tear it down.
3. Adoption of self-help neighborhoods of the current Rio policy of organizing public housing projects as "neighborhood units" is needed. This policy means that primary schools, health clinics, market centres, and meeting places are constructed as part of the project in accordance with its expected population and services already available.
4. Experiments should be made in mass , duction of small and simple houses, departing to some extent from present minimum standards of space and amenities. Housing agencies in Rio would be understandable reluctant to take this step, buy they may have no choice if they are to reach the masses of the shanty towns. This type of policy is currently being followed in a new housing program in Mexico.
5. It should also be a policy objective that small houses intended for the lower income groups be combined in neighborhood units

with larger houses for families able to pay higher rents and with the kinds of community services mentioned above.

6. "Urban Renewal" programmes should be drawn up to the rehabilitate as far as possible neighborhoods of deteriorating housing and tenement slums. Such a programme should imply technical and material aid to the occupants, inspection and enforcement of maintenance obligations upon the owner of rented dwellings. Up to date, efforts to precent deterioration and rehabilitate existing houses have received surprisingly little attention in the city of Rio.
7. Efforts should be made to improve the efficiency of the building industry, both by training workers and experiments with prefabricated building components and cheaper building materials.
8. Public housing programmes should be coordinated with other types of programmes-community development in particular that are aimed at raising the earning capacity and the standard of living of families below the income levels served by public housing.
9. There is a need for system of land taxes that would discourage the holding of vacant land for speculative purposes, and for wider municipal power to purchase land. The city of Rio can gain incalculable advantages by acquiring land well in advance of needs, at low prices, eventually using part of if for housing projects. The city of Stockholm (Sweden) in particular has benefited from such a policy.

Future Research Directions

Empirical research on housing demand in developing countries has grown over the past decades. However, few have tried to capture the pattern of behaviour of households, spatially and across income and demographic groups and housing type. While the finding of our study have just touched the tip of the iceberg, these initial results give reasons for optimism in that econometric models developed for developing countries, may apply fairly well for the analysis of cities in developing countries. Based on this study we can make some recommendations for future research in this direction:

1. The present study could be expanded by incorporating other cities, thereby complementing an intra-urban analysis of Rio with an inter-city one.
2. There is a need to study the housing market structure in Rio. This will give us more clues on the housing choice process.
3. There is also a need to incorporate and correctly specify a price term. The study could be conducted in the framework of Hedonic Theory.

AFTERWORD:
Relevance of the Study for India*

Housing is a major urban problem in India. There are too many people to share too few resources. India has several Rio de Janeiros. And each decade, new ones are added to the growing pool. Calcutta, Bombay, Delhi and Madras are now mega-cities. Ten more million cities would become-megacities by the turn of the century, and many more are in the queue to become million cities. The growth of population is rather too fast for the urban infrastructure to cope with it. And what makes the situation worse is the fact that overwhelming majority of those who migrate to the city as also those who are born there are poor and unskilled. They cannot buy land and build a house. City for them is a resource to be exploited; not a place to live a decent life.

Rural-urban migration has another serious implication for housing. In rural areas land is not that serious a problem. All those who have resources to build a house, can get land and almost everyone has a house, small or big, good or bad. In urban areas, access to land is the most serious problem. Provision of drinking water, sanitation, employment, education, health and all that goes with the urban life is more problematic in cities. Added to all these is the fact that the very process of migration renders some homeless overnight. Thus an artificial need and demand for housing crops up.

To understand urban housing problem of India it is therefore essential to analyse the urbanisation process and the urban structure of the country.

---

* Note: This chapter was written jointly with Dr. Suresh Misra, Research Officer, Indian Institute of Public Administration, New Delhi.

Urbanisation in India

Urbanisation in India began late because of the late advent of Industrial Revolution. Even today India has only one quarter of its population in cities and hence in comparison to the developed countries, it is not a highly urbanised country. The urban problems faced by India, and for that matter, the other Third World countries are, however, not only acute but also unprecedented. Never before had so many people congregated in a few urban centres with so inadequate resource base. The cities which were designed to accommodate 100,000 persons are now forced to take care of 1,000,000 persons or more.

Urbanisation in India in the past was slow and cyclical. Not more than ten per cent of population ever lived in cities in the pre-colonial times. Cities were not the manufacturing centres as such; they were centres of administration, commerce, and a few very specialised industries catering to the needs of the rich and nobles. Production of agricultural and industrial goods was the function of villages. And hence the employment opportunities were also in villages. City was a clean place, as were the villages.

The British changed this spatial structure of India's economy. The rural industries lost the ground and new spatial structure with a few port towns and capital cities specialising in the handling of raw materials for export, and the distribution in the country of finished products from abroad and later in the manufacture of cotton textiles was superimposed.

In due course, the new pattern of urbanisation was strengthened through urban industrialisation and rapid rural-urban migration of labour. The cities grew beyond their capacity to handle people and activities and reached a stage where they became dens of vices, crime, filth and unhealthy life on the one hand, and the only centres of manufacturing on the other.

According to the 1991 Census India has 4689 places designated as towns. These towns have been grouped into 3768 urban agglomerations (an agglomeration includes adjoining towns within the influence of a larger town forming a continuous spread). The total urban population amounts to 217 million i.e. 25.72 per cent of the total. The problems can be gauged from the fact that between 1901 and 1991, a period of 90 years the number of urban agglomerations and towns just doubled it was 1827 in (1901), but the population living therein increased by nine times (25.85 to 217.17 million). Further details of the trends of urbanisation in India is given in Table 8.1.

TABLE 8.1: Trend of Urbanisation in India

Census year	Number of UAs/Towns	Total population	Urban population	Urban population as percentage of total population	Decennial growth rate of urban population (per cent)	Tempo of Urbanisation (Per cent per year)		
						Annual exponential growth rate	Annual gain in percentage of urban population	Annual rate of gain in percentage of urban population
1	2	3	4	5	6	7	8	9
1901	1,827	238,396,327	25,851,873	10.84	...	...	...	...
1911	1,815	252,093,390	25,941,633	10.29	0.35	0.03	-0.06	-0.51
1921	1,949	251,321,213	28,086,167	11.18	8.27	0.79	0.09	0.86
1931	2,072	278,977,238	33,455,989	11.99	19.12	1.75	0.08	0.72
1941	2,250	318,660,580	44,153,297	13.86	31.97	2.77	0.19	1.56
1951	2,843	361,088,090	62,443,709	17.29	41.42	3.47	0.34	2.47
1961	2,365	439,234,771	78,936,603	17.97	26.41	2.34	0.07	0.41
1971	2,590	548,159,652	109,113,977	19.91	38.23	3.21	0.19	1.08
1981	3,378	683,329,097	159,462,547	23.34	46.14	3.83	0.34	1.72
1991	3,768	844,324,222	217,177,625	25.72	36.19	3.09	0.24	1.02

Notes: 1. As the 1981 Census was not conducted in Assam, the 1981 population figures for India include interpolated figures for Assam.

2. The 1991 Census has not been held in Jammu and Kashmir. The 1991 population figures for India include projected figures for Jammu and Kashmir as projected by the Standing Committee of Experts on Population Projections (October, 1989).

The urban structure of the country as indicated by size-class distribution of towns on the one hand and the pattern of growth of different classes of towns was clearly small town oriented in the early stages of urbanisation. These towns were quite spread out areawise and had less than 100,000 population. As industrialisation proceeded and the rural areas lost their industrial base the small towns gave way to large cities. The population of class V and VI towns, for example, declined from 26.24 per cent in 1901 to 2.89 per cent of the total urban population in 1991. And share of towns of class V and VI in the total number of towns declined from 66.53 per cent in 1901 to 25.22 per cent of total urban population in 1991 (Tables 8.2A, 8.2B and 8.2C).

Ninety years back in 1901, Calcutta alone had more than one million people. Between 1901 and 1941 only one more city was added to the million cities list i.e. Bombay. The 1951 census return showed up five such cities i.e. Calcutta, Bombay, Madras, Delhi and Hyderabad. The number increased to nine in 1971, to twelve in 1981 and to twenty three in 1991.

Housing Problem : How Acute It is?

The present housing shortage in India amounts to 27 million units — 19.5 million units in rural areas and 7.5 million units in urban areas. By the turn of this century the shortage is likely to grow to 40 million units i.e. 30 million in rural areas and 10 million units in urban areas. It is this shortage of 10 million units which is the concern of this chapter. It must however, be kept in view that urban problems cannot be seen in isolation. Quite often they are linked to the rural problem. In the case of housing, it is definitely so, because it is the rural-urban migration which is the major cause of housing shortage in Indian cities.

The older parts of Indian cities are over congested and over burdened often beyond recovery, and the newer parts have spread out far beyond the reach of urban infrastructure. In these peripheries are also located most of the shanty towns otherwise known as *jhopad pattis, jhuggi jhopadis* etc. Added to these housing and infrastructural problems is the environmental pollution caused by the polluting industrial and transport technologies.

As in 1981, 24.9 million housing units were available for 29.3 million urban households in India leaving a gap of 4.4 million units. It included of 3.1 million units of *kutcha* (mud) houses. Assuming that each household requires a house, the difference between number of

TABLE 8.2A: Urban Population by Size Class—India*, 1901-1991

Census year	All Classes	Class I	Class II	Class III	Class IV	Class V	Class VI
1	2	3	4	5	6	7	8
1901	25,616,051 $	6,661,100	2,892,094	4,006,520	5,334,969	5,158,901	1,562,467
1911	25,580,199 $	7,029,991	2,687,541	4,195,318	5,047,376	4,940,574	1,679,399
1921	27,691,306 $	8,224,720	2,878,025	4,409,381	5,063,414	5,170,671	1,945,095
1931	32,976,018 $	10,289,597	3,842,082	5,540,657	5,935,421	5,651,501	1,716,760
1941	43,558,665 $	16,651,745	4,975,530	7,123,533	6,872,240	6,566,116	1,369,501
1951	61,629,646 #	27,506,519	6,136,734	9,688,132	8,398,871	7,992,923	1,906,467
1961	77,562,000	39,882,780	8,712,782	13,138,936	9,902,236	5,328,762	596,504
1971	106,966,534	61,225,798	11,679,940	17,125,811	11,706,334	4,755,659	472,992
1981	156,419,768	94,503,745	18,189,728	22,409,119	14,930,267	5,603,015	783,894
1991	212,867,337	138,801,945	23,309,167	28,079,305	16,531,064	5,532,033	613,823

* Excludes Assam and Jammu & Kashmir.

$ Excludes Population of six towns in 1941 four each in 1931 and 1921 and two each in 1911 and 1901 of Goa as their population could not be ascertained.

\# Excludes population of 12,019 of Kanchrapara Rural Development Colony which gave place to Kalyan and Gayeshpur Government Colony towns of Nadia District of West Bengal in 1961. Separate figures for 1951 of Kalyani and Gayeshpur Government Colony (Portions) are not available. Therefore these figures have not been included in any class of towns.

TABLE 8.2B: Percentage Distribution of Urban Population by Size Class—India, 1901-1991

Census year	All classes	I	II	III	IV	V	VI
1	2	3	4	5	6	7	8
1901	100.00	26.00	11.29	15.64	20.83	20.14	6.10
1911	100.00	27.48	10.51	16.40	19.73	19.31	6.57
1921	100.00	29.70	10.39	15.92	18.29	18.67	7.03
1931	100.00	31.20	11.65	16.80	18.00	17.14	5.21
1941	100.00	38.23	11.42	16.35	15.78	15.08	3.14
1951	100.00	44.63	9.96	15.72	13.63	12.97	3.09
1961	100.00	51.42	11.23	16.94	12.77	6.87	0.77
1971	100.00	57.24	10.92	16.01	10.94	4.45	0.44
1981	100.00	60.42	11.63	14.33	9.54	3.58	0.50
1991	100.00	65.20	10.95	13.19	7.77	2.60	0.29

Note: Based on data contained in Statement 16.

TABLE 8.2C: Percentage Distribution of Urban Agglomerations/Towns by Size Class—India, 1901-1991

Census year	All classes	I	II	III	IV	V	VI
1	2	3	4	5	6	7	8
1901	100.00	1.33	2.37	7.18	21.59	41.08	26.45
1911	100.00	1.31	2.28	7.70	20.75	40.31	27.65
1921	100.00	1.53	2.38	7.66	19.53	38.75	30.15
1931	100.00	1.73	2.78	9.07	21.52	39.66	25.24
1941	100.00	2.24	3.38	11.05	22.74	42.01	18.58
1951	100.00	2.72	3.26	11.70	21.75	40.21	20.36
1961	100.00	4.49	5.68	19.25	31.68	31.32	7.58
1971	100.00	5.98	6.99	22.53	33.40	25.16	5.94
1981	100.00	6.66	8.32	22.74	32.45	22.77	7.06
1991	100.00	8.20	9.45	25.68	31.45	20.09	5.13

households and houses indicates the unsatisfied demand. The gap in 1981 was 1.3 million units excluding, 3.1 million *kutcha* houses. 0.2 million households with 0.62 million people were without any shelter. They lived on pavements, etc. The rest i.e. 1.1 million shared accommodations with others and overcrowded the living space.

Apart from the shortage of housing units noted above a fairly good percentage of existing structures are too old to be safe and liveable. In 1981, 1.2 million units (4.2 per cent of the total stock) were more than 80 years old. If these houses are excluded from the total stock, the shortage amounts to 5.6 million units. Added to this shortage is the overcrowding. Three or more persons per room amount to crowding, 47.80 per cent of the urban households live in crowded and unhealthy living conditions.

The 1981 census data pertaining to housing show that the vast majority of *kutcha* (mud) and semi-*pucca* houses were devoid of electricity, water supply, toilet, bathroom, etc. And not all the *pucca* (brick) houses had these basic facilities. On the whole, only 52.2 per cent of the units had the above facilities leaving 13.4 million houses without them.

Thus the urban housing backlog in India as on March 1, 1981 amounted to 5.9 million units (Table 8.3). It stands at 9 to 10 million units in 1992.

TABLE 8.3: Urban Housing Need (backlog) in India in 1981

(in million units)

1.	(a)	Houseless	0.2
2.	(a)	Overcrowding and Congestion	1.1
	(b)	Number of married couples requiring separate room/houses	0.3
	(c)	Replacement of kutcha houses	3.1
	(d)	Obsolescence/replacement of old houses	1.2
		Total	5.9

Housing in Metropolitan Cities

The housing problem is more acute in larger towns, as the pressure of population on land is higher there. The phenomenal increase in the number and population of larger towns is thus one of the major causes of the accentuation of housing problem in India.

Overcrowding is the hall mark of India's growing cities. In 1981, urban India consisted of 29.3 million households. Majority of these households (64.89%) are concentrated in class I cities i.e. cities with 100,000 or more people. This high concentration gets further accentuated because 50.57 per cent of the population of class I cities is located in 23 metropolitan urban agglomerations (Table 8.4).

TABLE 8.4: Distribution of Class I Urban Agglomerations/Cities (Population 100,000 and above) by Different Population Sizes in India, 1991

Population size		No. of UAs/ Cities	Population			Percentage of population of Class I UAs/Cities	Sex ratio
			Persons	Males	Females		
1		2	3	4	5	6	7
	CLASS I	300	149,730,050	74,248,492	65,481,558	100.00	882
M1	Less than 200,000	167	22,939,086	11,990,866	10,948,220	16.42	913
M2	200,000—299,999	40	9,606,814	5,045,392	4,561,422	6.88	904
M3	300,000—499,999	40	15,586,157	8,178,998	7,407,159	11.15	906
M4	500,000—999,999	30	20,936,734	11,128,685	9,808,049	14.98	881
M5	1,000,000 and above	23	70,661,259	37,904,551	32,756,708	50.57	864
	(i) 1,000,000—1,999,999	*14*	*17,175,849*	*9,127,058*	*8,048,791*	*12.29*	*882*
	(ii) 2,000,000—4,999,999	*5*	*16,260,762*	*8,571,965*	*7,688,797*	*11.64*	*897*
	(iii) 5,000,000 and above	*4*	*37,224,648*	*20,205,528*	*17,019,120*	*26.64*	*842*

Note: Excludes Jammu and Kashmir where Census has not been held.

The housing problems of metropolitan areas differ from the rest of the urban areas in terms of both nature and magnitude. Each metro has a million or more population. According to the 1981 census, the twelve metropolitan cities had 41 million population, 8 million households and 7.74 million houses. Out of these, 0.25 million households had no separate house and 0.075 million households were houseless.

Only 60 per cent of households had water supply within the premises 70.6 per cent had electricity, and 72.5 per cent had toilets.

Taking the houseless households without separate housing units, kutcha houses needing replacement, and obsolescence together, the metropolitan housing shortage as in 1981 was of the order of 1.25 million units (Table 8.5).

TABLE 8.5: Housing Needs in Metropolitan Areas in India in 1981

	Components	Number
1.	Shelterless	75,000
2.	Households without separate houses (overcrowding)	1,78,000
3.	Kutcha houses	6,71,000
4.	Obsolescence (4.2 per cent as in the case of urban stock)	3,25,000
	Total	12,49,000

The total urban housing gap of 5.9 million units is likely to further widen in years to come. Projections made in mid eighties amount to 7.5 million units by 2001 AD (Table 8.6)

TABLE 8.6: Urban Housing Projections for India (as on 31 March) in millions

Year	1981	1986	1991	1996	2001	
	29.3	34.4	39.5	44.6	49.7	Urban households
	28.0	32.8	37.5	42.3	47.0	Housing stock
	23.4	28.0	32.6	37.4	42.2	Acceptable housing stock

The most recent projections however, indicate a gap of 9.5 million units by 2001 AD. Proportionately larger share of this shortage will be in the metropolitan cities particularly in the megacities.

When we look at the qualitative aspects, the situation is equally alarming. Most of the houses in the older parts of the city are unsafe, dingy and highly congested. This is particularly the case with rented houses. The rents are low and fixed under the rent control act. While these acts were designed to give security to tenants, they were obvious of the fact that houses needed repairs which could not be done without economic rent. Low rents led to low or no investment in repairs. As the condition of houses deteriorated, the space was subdivided and poor were brought as sub-tenants. In due course the central part of the city, once a place of the rich, became a slum (Table 8.7).

TABLE 8.7: Percentage of Households by Availability of Electricity and Toilet Facility in India

Metro towns/ UTs	URBAN					
	Electricity			Toilet		
	Total	Owners	Tenants	Total	Owners	Tenants
1. Hyderabad	71.7	67.6	75.1	69.6	63.5	74.5
2. Ahmedabad	75.8	82.6	70.5	73.9	82.1	67.7
3. Bangalore	72.3	66.6	75.4	56.3	64.7	52.2
4. Bombay	77.6	72.7	80.3	73.4	70.7	75.1
5. Pune	76.1	66.2	80.8	59.9	53.4	66.9
6. Nagpur	69.8	68.5	71.2	68.6	60.9	72.3
7. Jaipur	78.6	70.3	90.5	75.1	71.9	87.6
8. Madras	65.4	56.0	71.1	69..7	55.0	78.6
9. Kanpur	62.5	56.8	65.0	63.7	57.4	66.5
10. Lucknow	66.8	65.8	68.7	65.6	63.4	70.0
11. Calcutta	62.9	59.8	64.9	86.0	83.4	87.6
12. Delhi	75.1	69.9	80.5	68.2	62.1	74.5
Total	70.9			72.5		

Then there are shanty towns or *jhopad pattis* created by the poor both inside and outside the municipal limits often illegally occupying vacant institutional or private land. These consist of temporary shanties or hutments made of local materials like bamboo, tin sheets, mud, and plastic sheets. The police authorities eject and throw them out, and at times even prosecute them but these punitive measures do not deter the poor and needy from coming again. In due course they form an association which is affiliated to a political party to protect themselves from police 'brutality' as they call it. It takes a decade or so before the colony is semi-permanently secure.

In these urban slums and shanty towns, the shelter situation is really precarious but what makes the situation worse is the lack of civic amenities like electricity, sewage, waste disposal, education and medicare. The inhabitants are usually engaged in the informal sector of the urban economy. Their incomes are low. But even if the incomes increase, there is no opportunity to invest in housing. The municipal services cannot reach them because of the illegal character of the colonies. Inhabitants cannot invest because they have no land title. Each year new blighted colonies crop up around the centre of the city, and in the urban periphery. And thus the situation worsens while the remedial measures get entangled in the legal and bureaucratic maize.

Urban Housing Supply

Dependable data on urban housing supply are not available. Public works department and municipal corporations, housing boards and development authorities are the sources of whatever data one can get. The National Building Organisation gets the PWD data on value of work done, number of units constructed, floor area added etc. The municipalities furnish data relating to private sector houses/building, number of housing plans sanctioned, and completion certificates granted, etc. Unfortunately, the small towns with less than 10,000 population are not covered by these data.

The NSS (National Sample Survey Organisation) conducted a survey for NBO in 1972-74. Thereafter, the only source of housing data is the decennial population cènsus which gets to the public far too late to be of much policy and planning use.

The total housing stock of the metropolitan cities was 14.1 million units in 1961, 18.5 million units in 1971 and 27.6 million units in 1981. Thus during 1961-71, 4.4 million units, and during 1971-81 9.1 million new houses were added to the housing stock. This amounts to 7.1 houses per 1000 population.

If one takes only *pucca* houses into account, the growth rate was 81.5 per cent during 1961-71, and 53.4 per cent during 1971-81. Thus the rate of construction in effect declined from 5.6 per cent in 1961-71 per cent to 4.7 per cent in 1971-81.

According to the Fifth Five Year Plan (1975-80), India was to construct 1.2 million houses each year to cover the backlog and cater to the needs of the new entrants to the urban housing market. This amounted to 10 housing units per 1000 population. Only 3.5 units per

1000 population were however added to the housing stock annually leaving a gap of 6.5 units per 1000 population.

The structural details of the houses are also available from the decennial census. Of the 28 million houses in 1981, 18.1 million were *pucca*, 6.8 million semi-*pucca* and 3.1 million *kutcha* (Table 8.8A). Out of the 9.5 million houses that have been added during 1971-81, 6.3 million were *pucca* and 2.5 million semi-*pucca*. The NSS data show progressive conversion of *kutcha* and semi-*pucca* houses into *pucca* houses (Table 8.8B).

TABLE 8.8A: Distribution of Urban Residential Houses by Type of Structures in India

(in millions)

Type of structure	1961	1971	1981*
Pucca	6.5 (46.0)	11.8 (63.8)	18.1 (64.6)
Semi-*pucca*	4.9 (35.0)	4.3 (23.5)	6.8 (24.3)
Kutcha	2.7 (19.0)	2.4 (12.7)	3.1 (11.1)
Total	14.1 (100.0)	18.4 (100.0)	28.0 (100.0)

* Includes estimated figures for Assam. Figures in brackets are percentages.

TABLE 8.2B: Percentage Distribution of Households by Type of Structures in India

Type of structure	1953-54	1964-65	1973-74
Pucca	27.64	52.75	64.52
Semi-*pucca*	38.97	17.19	19.64
Kutcha	24.49	29.95	15.84
Others	8.30	0.11	
Total	100.00	100.00	100.00

Source: NSSO's Rounds 26, 195 and Sarvekshana Vol. I, No. 2, 1977.

The census figures show that in 1961-71, 5.3 million *pucca* units were added. This increased to 6.3 million units in 1971-81. As regards semi-*pucca* units, the number declined by 6 lakh units during 1961-71 and increased by only 2.5 million units in 1971-81. The *kutcha* units also declined by 3 lakh units in 1961-71. Many of the semi-*pucca* and *kutcha* houses were converted into *pucca* houses.

The major governmental agencies supplying urban housing are central public works department, post and telegraph, armed forces, railways, autonomous institutions like universities, financial institutions like Life Insurance Corporation, police, research institutions, state governments and local self government agencies. These together supplied 1.806 million units in 1981. The social housing scheme provided 0.604 million units; the cooperative sector 0.626 million units and the private corporations 0.271 million units, making the 1981 total supply of 3.357 million units. It is estimated that in 1986 the government sector's contribution increased from 1.805 to 2.258 million units. On prorata basis, the government sector supply should stand at 2.50 million units and the total supply at approximately 5 million units in 1991.

Urban Housing Policy

The Urban Housing Policy in India has veered round three strategies until 1990. One was designed to protect the tenants from eviction and exorbitant rent, the other to improve existing houses and public utilities, and last, to add to the existing housing stock. There has been some change in these strategies during the past few years. The rent control acts of various states are being modified so that the owners have the incentive to invest in the improvement of the buildings. Nothing meaningful has yet happened but the trends are in favour of relaxation of the rigidities. Considerable efforts are on to improve the living conditions in urban slums and shanty towns. Several national and international agencies are contributing to the programmes and projects designed to improve the housing conditions both in urban and rural areas. And as noted earlier, several national agencies including financial institutions are involved in the construction of new houses also.

The new houses being build in urban centres of India have not yet benefitted the low-income and poor households. They cater to the needs of the high and middle income groups. Among the poor, only those who have salaried income have benefitted from these schemes. The informal sector workers, the casual income households, and factory labour, and footpath peddlers do not have access to the houses constructed under these schemes.

Even those who have benefitted from the new housing schemes, are not necessarily satisfied with the quality of supply. No systematic surveys have been conducted to know what different groups of households needed. What the households need and desire to have, has been assessed by the planners and architects according to their own perception of housing needs and wants.

As a result, more resources go in the creation of housing stock which is not what people need or want to have. If the people's need are better understood, more houses can be provided in less amount of investment. What is needed is a policy outline to encourage people to build their own houses rather than to try to give ready made houses. Secondly, there are serious limitations to official agencies supplying housing. The cooperative and private sectors must enter the field and housing should be declared as industry and receive the same facilities which other industries get. India should not lose sight of the fact that housing accounted for 16.72 per cent of the gross capital formation in the country in 1984-85.

Relevance of the Rio Study

There are a number of lessons that one can learn from Rio study reported earlier to solve housing problems in Indian cities. The first lesson is the survey to better assess the housing needs as perceived by the people themselves. The idea that planners, and architects because of their professional training know the needs better, is patently wrong. A systematic survey is urgently needed. It could be organised by the NBO through the NSSO or similar other relevant organisations.

The second lesson one learns is the preference of the low and middle income households to have larger houses as income increases. For these households, if the choice is between a small apartment and a plot of land where they can build their houses incrementally, they would choose the latter. This means that given the current resource crunch, there is no point in trying to build houses for the people. People can build their houses if they have access to land. Public investment should go in the provision of land, basic amenities, and social services.

Land has now become a major source of black money and speculation in India's large cities. The urban fringe is now converted into farm houses and purchased for speculative purposes depriving the farmers of their land at a very low price. The official agencies are not able to put to stop this process. It is now the time for them to concentrate on land acquisition and distribution of land to the needy households. The other area of concentration is infrastructure. The cooperative and private agencies should work with the official agencies to achieve this objective.

The other conclusions of the study are Rio specific and hence may not be equally relevant to other Third World Cities. Nevertheless, they should not be ignored while formulating urban housing policies. For example, older people prefer apartment to large houses. This would probably be a universal phenomenon particularly because the days of helps and servants and security for life and property in large cities are now practically gone. It would not be a unwise policy to invest in small apartments which are within the reach of the middle and low income group people in the age group 50 and above.

REFERENCES

Census of India, *India Part II Special, 1981 Series.*

Census of India, *Primary Census Abstract General Population, Part II B (i).*

Census of India, Provisional Population Total : Rural-Urban *Distribution*, Paper 2 of 1991.

Central Statistical Organisation (CSO) : *National Accounts Statistics*, January, 1986.

Dwendra B. Gupta, *Urban Housing in India*, World Bank Staff Working Paper No. 730.

G.C. Mathur, "Analysis of Housing Requirements in India" Paper presented to the National Commission on Urbanisation, 1982.

Government of India, *Handbook of Housing Statistics* 1982-83 (NB).

Planning Commission *Seventh Five Year Plan.*

Town and Country Planning Organisation, *Urban Statistics*, January, 1986.

United Nations, *Methods of Estimating Housing Needs*, UN Series F.No.12.

APPENDIX A

MAXIMUM LIKELIHOOD ESTIMATION

The author has used maximum likelihood estimation technique to econometrically infer the parameters of $B_1 \ldots B_k$ from a sample of observations. In this appendix the maximum likelihood estimation technique is explained in detail. The discussion is restricted to the most typical case where data consists of individuals drawn at random from a population.

The maximum likelihood method of obtaining estimates of parameters is based on the notion that a sample of values we observe is more likely to come from some population than from others. If we can characterize observations from a population as having a particular probability distribution, then some values of the parameters characterizing the distribution are more likely to have generated the sample than others. The maximum likelihood estimates of the parameters of the probability distribution function are the values that maximize the likelihood function, defined to be joint probability distribution functions of the observed random sample and interpreted as a function of the unknown parameters given the sample values.

Here we will discuss a multinomial logit model only. As it will be shown, logit has some special properties that under certain circumstances greatly simplify estimation of its parameters. Most of this theory is attributable to McFadden (1974). Let N denote the sample size and define:

$$Y_{in}$$

The likelihood function for a general multinomial choice model is:

$$L^{*} = \prod_{n=1}^{n} \prod_{i \in C_n} P_n(i)^{Y_{in}} \qquad (1)$$

Where for a linear in parameters logit

$$P_n(i) = \frac{e^{\beta' X_{in}}}{\sum_j inC_n e^{\beta' X_{in}}} \tag{2}$$

Taking the logarithm of Equation 1, we seek a maximum of:

$$L = \sum_{i=1}^{N} \sum_{i \in C_n} Y_{in}\left(\beta' X_{in} - \ln \sum_{i \in C_n} e^{\beta' X_{jn}}\right) \tag{3}$$

Setting the first derivatives of L with respect to the coefficients equal to zero, we can obtain the necessary first-order conditions:

$$\frac{\partial L}{\partial \beta_k} = \sum_{n=1}^{N} \sum_{i \in C_n} Y_{in}(X_{ink} - \left[\frac{\sum_{j \in C_n} e^{\beta' X_{jn}} X_{jnk}}{\sum_{j \in C_n} e^{\beta' X_{jn}}}\right] = 0 \text{ For } k = 1..K \tag{4}$$

OR

$$\sum_{n=1}^{N} \sum_{i \in C_n} [Y_{in} - P_n(i)]X_{ink} = 0 \text{ For } K = 1...K \tag{5}$$

The second derivative of L are give by:

$$\frac{\partial^2 L}{\partial \beta_k \partial \beta_i} = \sum_{n=1}^{N} \sum_{i \in C_n} P_n(i)\left[X_{ink} - \sum_{j \in C_n} XjnkP_n(j)\right].$$

$$\left[X_{in1} - \sum_{j \in C_n} X_{jn1} P_n(j)\right] \tag{6}$$

Under relatively weak conditions McFadden (1974) has shown that L in Equation 3 is globally concave, so if a solution to Equation 5 exists, it is unique. The maximum likelihood estimator of B is consistent, asystematically normal and asystematically efficient.

The first-order condition for Equation 5 can be written as:

$$\frac{1}{N}\sum_{n=1}^{N} \sum_{i \in C_n} Y_{in} X_{ink} = \frac{1}{N}\sum_{n=1}^{N} \sum_{i \in C_n} P_n(i) X_{ink'} \quad k = 1..K$$

This means that the average value of an attribute for the chosen alternatives is equal to the average value predicted by estimated choice probabilities.

BIBLIOGRAPHY

Amemiya, T. (1978). "On the Two-Step Estimation of a Multinomial Logit Model," *Journal of Econometrics,* 8, 13-21.

Amemiya, Takeshi (1981). "Qualitative Response Models: A Survey," *Journal of Economic Literature,* 19, 1483-1536.

Anas, A. (1980). "A Probabilistics Approach to the Structure of Rental Housing Markets," *Journal of Urban Economics,* 7, 225-247.

Anas, A. (1981). "The Estimation of Multinomial Logit Models of Joint Location and Travel Mode Choice From Aggregated Data," *Journal of Regional Science,* 21, 223-242.

Anas, A. (1982). *Residential Location Markets and Urban Transportation: Economic Theory, Econometrics, and Policy Analysis with Discrete Choice Models,* Academic Press Publishing Company, New York.

Andrikopoulos, A.A. and J.A. Brox (1984). "The Urban Housing Market: A New Approach for Estimating Demand for Housing by Dwelling Type," *Journal of Urban Economics,* 15, 12: 230-243.

Arcangeli, E. Fabio, Giorgio Leonardi and Aura Reggiana (1985). "Alternative Theoretical Frameworks for the Interpretation of Random Utility Models," *Papers of the Regional Science Association,* 58, 7-20.

Atherton, T.J. and M.E. Ben-Akiva (1976). "Transferability and Updating of Disaggregated Travel Demand Models," *Transportation Research Record,* 610, 12-18.

Awan, J., J. Odling-Smec, et al. "Household Attributes and the Demand for Private Rental Housing," *Economica,* 49, 183-200.

Awan, K., J. Odling-Smec and C. Whitehead (1982). "Household Attributes and the Demand for Private Rental Housing," *Economica,* 498, 183-200.

Barbosa, E. (1985). "Housing the Urban Poor in Rio-de-Janeiro: The Loteamento Populares," Unpublished Ph.D. Dissertation, Dept. of Geography, Boston University, Boston, Massachusetts.

Becker, G.S. (1965). "The Theory of Allocation of Time," *Economic Journal,* 75, 493-517.

Ben-Akiva, M.E. (1973). "Structure of Passenger Travel Demand Models," Ph.D. Dissertation, Massachusetts Institute of Technology, Deptt. of Civil Engineering, Cambridge, Massachusetts.

Ben-Akiva, M.E. (1974). "Structure of Passenger Travel Demand Models," *Transportation Research Record,* 526, 26-42.

Ben-Akiva, M.E. and S.R. Lerman (1979). "Disaggregate Travel and Mobility Choice Models and Measures of Accessibility," in D.A. Hensher and P.R. Stopher (eds.), *Behavioural Travel Modelling,* Croom Helm Publishing Company, London, The United Kingdom, England, 654-679.

Benus, J., K. Kmenta and H. Shapiro (1976). "The Dynamics of Household Budget Allocation to Food Expenditures," *Review of Economics and Statistics,* 58:2, 129-138.

Berkowitz, M.K. and G.H. Haines (1982). "Predicting Demand for Residential Solar Heating: An Attribute Method," *Management Science,* 28:7, 717-727.

Boehm, T. (1980). "Tenure Choice and Expected Mobility: A Synthesis," *Journal of Urban Economics,* 10, 375-389.

Borsch-Supan, A. (1986). "Household Formation, Housing Prices, and Public Policy Impacts," *Journal of Public Economics,* 25.

Borsch-Supan, A. (1987). "On the Compatibility of Nested Multinomial Logit Models With Utility Maximization," *Journal of Econometrics.*

Borsch-Supan, A. and J. Pitkin (1987). "On Discrete Choice Models of Housing Demand," *Journal of Urban Economics,* 21.

Cameron, Trudy Ann (1985). "A Nested Model of Energy Conservation Activity by Owners of Existing Single Family Dwellings," *Review of Economics and Statistics,* 67: 205-211.

Chatterjee, L. (1980). *Affordability of Housing in Nigeria,* The Free University, Amsterdam, The Netherlands.

Clark, W.A.V and K. Avery (1978). "Residential Preference: An Alternate View of Intra-Urban Space," *Environment and Planning,* 11, 689-704.

Clark, W.A.V. and J.L. Onaka (1985). "An Empirical Test of a Joint Model of Residential Mobility and Housing Choice," *Environment and Planning,* 17, 915-930.

Crow, Robert Thomas, Kan Hua Young and Thomas Cooley (1973). "Alternative Demand Functions for Abstract: Transportation Models," *Transportation Research,* 7, 335-354.

Currim, Imran S. (1982). "Predictive Testing of Consumer Choice Models Not Subject to Independence of Irrelevant Alternatives, *Journal of Marketing Research*, 19, 208-222.

Danganzo, C.F. (1979). *Multinomial Probit, The Theory, and Its Applications, to Demand Forecasting,* Academic Press Publishing Company, New York.

Debreu, G. (1960). "Review of R. Luce: Individual Choice Behavior," *American Economic Review,* 50, 186-188.

Diamond, D. (1980). "Income and Residential Location," *Urban Studies,* 17, 1-12.

Fischer, M. and E. Aufhauser, "Housing Choice in Regulated Markets," *A Nested Multinomial Logit Analysis,* Deptt. of Geography, University of Vienna.

Fischer, Manfred and Peter Nijkamp (1985). "Developments Explanatory Discrete Spatial Data and Choice Analysis," *Progress in Human Geography* 9:4, 515-551.

Fischer, Manfred and Peter Nijkamp (1987), from "Static Towards Dynamic Discrete Choice Modelling: A State of the Art Review," *Regional Science and Urban Economics,* 17, 3-27.

Follain, J. and E. Jimenez (1985). "The Demand for Housing Characteristics in Developing Countries," *Urban Studies,* 22, 421-432.

Follain, J., G. Lim, et al. (1980). "The Demand for Housing in Developing Countries: The Case of Korea," *Journal of Urban Economics,* 7, 313-336.

Gaudry, M.J.I. (1980). "Dogit and Logit Models of Paved Mode Choice in Montreal," *Canadian Journal of Economics,* 13, 268-279.

Goldberg, M. and P. Chinloy (1984). *Urban Land Economics,* John Wiley and Sons Publishing Company, New York.

Goodman, J. (1976). "Housing Consumption Disequilibrium and Local Residential Mobility," *Environment and Planning,* 8, 855-875.

Goodwin, S. (1977). "Measuring the Value of Housing Quality: A Note," *Journal of Regional Science,* 17, 1, 107-115.

Harsman, B. and Snickans (1976). "Disaggregated Housing Demand Models: Some Theoretical Approaches," *Papers of Regional Science Association,* 34, 121-143.

Hausman, Jerry A. and Daniel McFadden (1975). *Urban Travel demand: A Behavioral Analysis,* North Holland Publishing Company, Amsterdam, The Netherlands.

Hausman, J. and D. McFadden (1984). "Specification Tests for the Multinational Logit Model," *Econometrica,* 52(5), 1219-1240.

Hensher, D.A. and L.W. Johnson (1981). *Applied Discrete Choice Modelling,* Croom Helm Publishing Company, London, The United Kingdom, England.

Hinloopwa, E., P. Nijkamp, et al. (1983), "Qualitative Discrete Multiple Criteria Choice Models in Regional Planning," *Regional Science and Urban Economics,* 13(1), 77-102.

Horowitz, J. (1982). "Specification Tests for Probabilistic Choice Models," *Transportation Research,* 16A (5-6), 383-394.

Jain, Arun K., Franklin Acito, et al. (1979). "A Comparison of the Internal Validity of Alternative Parameter Estimation Methods in Decompositional Multiattribute Preference Models," *Journal of Marketing Research,* 16, 313-332.

King, A.T. (1980). "The Demand for Housing: A Lancastrian Approach," *Southern Economic Journal,* 43, 1077-1087.

Lancaster, Kelvin (1966). "A New Approach to Consumer Theory," *Journal of Political Economy,* 74, 132-157.

Lierap, W. Van and P. Nijkamp (984). "Perspectives of Disaggregate Choice Models on the Housing Market in D. Pitfield (ed.), *Discrete Choice Models in Regional Science,* Pion, London, 141-162.

Linneman, P. (1981). "The Demand for Residence Site Characteristics," *Journal of Urban Economics,* 9, 129-148.

Luce, R.D. (1959). *Individual Choice Behavior,* John Wiley and Sons Publishing Company, New York.

Luce, R.D. and P. Suppes (1965). "Preference, Utility and Subjective Probability" in *Handbook of Mathematical Psychology,* Volume III, John Wiley and Sons Publishing Company, New York.

Maddala, G.S. (1977). *Econometrics,* McGraw-Hill, New York.

Maisel, J., J. Burnham et al. (1971). "The Demand for Housing: A Comment," *Review of Economics and Statistics,* 53, 4, 410-413.

Malpezzi, S. and S. Mayo (1987). "The Demand for Housing in Developing Countries: Empirical Estimates from Household Data," *Economic Development and Cultural Change,* 2, 687-721.

Mayo, S. (1981). "Theory and Estimation in the Economics of Housing Demand," *Journal of Urban Economics,* 10, 95-116.

McCarthy, K. (1976). "The Household Life Cycle and Housing Choice," *Papers of Regional Science Association,* 55-80.

McCarthy, Patrick S. (1977). "Residential Location and the Journey to Work: An Empirical Analysis," *Journal of Transportation Economics and Policy,* 11, 169-184.

McFadden, Daniel, (1973). "Conditional Logit Analysis of Qualitative Choice Behavior," in Paul Zarembka (ed.), *Frontiers in Econometrics,* Academic Press Publishing Company, New York, New York.

McFadden, D.L., K. Train, et al. (1977), "An Application of Diagnostic Tests for the Independence From Irrelevant Alternative Property of the Multinomial Logit Model," *Transportation Research Record,* 637, 39-46.

McFadden, Daniel (1978). "Modeling the Choice of Residential Location in Karlquist, A.L. Lundavist, F. Snikars, and J.W. Weibull (eds.), *Spatial Interaction Theory and Planning Models,* North Holland Publishing Company, Amsterdam, The Netherlands, pp. 75-96.

Mills, E. (1972). *Studies in the Structure of the Urban Economy,* Johns Hopkins University Press, Baltimore, Maryland.

Musgrave, P. (1978). *Consumer Behavior in Latin America,* Brookings Institute, Washington, D.C.

Muth, R.F. (1966). "Household Production and Consumer Demand Functions," *Econometrica,* 34, 699-708.

Nijkamp, P. (1979). "Gravity and Empty Models: The State of the Art," in *New Developments in Modelling Travel Demand and Urban Systems,* Saxon House Publishing Company, Farnborough, The United Kingdom, England, 281-319.

Onaka, J. (1983). "A Multiple Attribute Housing Disequilibrium Model of Residential Mobility," *Environment and Planning,* 15, 751-765.

Onaka, J. and W.A.V. Clark (1983). "A Disaggregate Model of Residential Mobility and Housing Choice," *Geographical Analysis,* 15, 287-304.

Ortuzar, J. deD. (1983). "Nested Logit Models for Mixed-Mode Travel in Urban Corridors," *Transportation Research,* 17A, 283-299.

Pirie, G.M. (1976). "Thoughts on Revealed Preference and Spacial Behavior," *Environment and Planning,* 8, 947-955.

Pitfield, D.E. ed. (1974). *Discrete Choice Models in Regional Science,* Pion, The United Kingdom, England.

Portes, A. (1979). "Housing Policy, Urban Poverty, and the State: The Favelas of Rio de Janeiro: 1972-1976," *Latin American Research Review,* 14, 2, 3-24.

Quigley, J.M. (1985). "Consumer Choice of Dwelling, Neighbourhood and Public Services," *Regional Science and Urban Economics,* 15, 41-63.

Rosen, Sherwin (1974). "Hedonic Prices and Implicit Markets: Product Differentiation in Pure Competition," *Journal of Political Economy,* 82, 34-55.

Rushtan, G. (1969). "Analysis of Spatial Behavior By Revealed Space Preference," *Annals of the Association of American Geographers,* 59, 391-400.

Small, K.A. and D. Brownstone (1982). "Efficient Estimation of Nested Logit Models: An Application to Trip Planning," Princeton University, Princeton, New Jersey, Economic Research Program, Research Memorandum 296.

Smith, T.R. and W.A.V. Clark (1982). "Housing Market Search Behavior and Expected Utility Theory I: Measuring Preference for Housing," *Environment and Planning,* 14, 681-698.

Straszheim, M.R. (1973). "Estimation of the Demand for Urban Housing Services from Household Survey Data," *Review of Economics and Statistics,* 55, 1-8.

Takayama, T. and G.G. Judge (1972). *Spatial and Temporal Price and Allocation Models,* North Holland Publishing Company, Amsterdam, The Netherlands.

Timmermans, M.J.P. (1984). "Decompositional Multiattribute Preference Models in Specified Choice Analysis: A Review of Some Recent Developments," *Progress in Human Geography,* 8:2, 189-221.

Train, K. (1986). *Qualitative Choice Analysis: Theory, Econometrics and Application to Automobile Demand,* Massachusetts Institute of Technology Press, Cambridge, Massachusetts.

Tversky, A. (1972). "Elimination by Aspects: A Theory of Choice," *Psychological Review,* 79(4), 281-299.

Vetter, D.M. and A.M. Brasileiro (1978). "Towards a Development Strategy for Grande Rio de Janeiro," *Latin American Urban Research,* 6, 259-279:6.

Vetter, D.M. (1975). *The Impact of Metropolitan System on the Interpersonal and Spatial Distribution of Real and Monetary Income: The Case of Grande Rio*«MDUL, Comparative Urban

Studies, School of Architecture and Urban Planning, University of California at Los Angeles.

Vetter, D.M. (1982). "Per Capita Income as a Measure of Family Income and Its Variation Over the Family Life Cycle," Mimeograph, IBGE, Rio de Janeiro, Brazil.

Wheaton, W. (1977). "A Bid Rent Approach to Housing Demand," *Journal of Urban Economics*, 200-217.

Williams, R.C. (1979). "A Logit Model of Demand for Neighborhood," in D. Segel (ed.), *The Economics of Neighborhood*, Academic Press, New York, 17-42.

Wilson, A.G., R.H. Rees and C.M. Leigh (1977). *Models of Cities and Regions: Theoretical and Empirical Developments,* John Wiley and Sons Publishing Company, London, The United Kingdom, England.

INDEX